SAVING LIVES: SIR ARTHUR CONAN DOYLE AND THE CAMPAIGN FOR BODY ARMOUR, 1914–18

T0345521

SAVING LIVES: SIR ARTHUR CONAN DOYLE AND THE CAMPAIGN FOR BODY ARMOUR, 1914–18

Philip Abbott

ROYAL ARMOURIES

TALKING POINTS SERIES

Published by Royal Armouries Museum, Armouries Drive, Leeds LS10 1LT, United Kingdom

www.royalarmouries.org

ISBN 978 0 948092 82 4

Edited by Martyn Lawrence
Designed by Out of House Publishing

Printed by W&G Baird
A CIP record for this book is available from the British Library

CONTENTS

ILLUSTRATIONS

PLATES

PREFACE

This work has been inspired by a small collection of letters, some from serving soldiers, some from private individuals, and some from commercial manufacturers, that were sent to Sir Arthur Conan Doyle in response to his efforts to persuade the authorities to provide British soldiers with protection against shrapnel, and rifle and machine gun fire, during the First World War. It seeks to place the collection in the context of the wider public campaign that began in the press in 1915, following the heavy losses experienced during the German offensive in Flanders and the Allied counter-offensive in Artois, and resumed in 1916 as news of the terrible casualties suffered during the Battle of the Somme became known. It examines Conan Doyle's personal motives for taking part in the debate, and investigates the part he played together with another Edinburgh graduate, Dr Caleb Saleeby, in promoting the development of helmets, body armour and shields. It asks whether they were successful in influencing official policy, and reveals what the War Office and Ministry of Munitions were actually doing to provide better protection for the troops. It examines some of the body shields that were commercially manufactured, and the official body armour that was eventually produced as a result of extensive tests and field trials.

ACKNOWLEDGEMENTS

The author wishes to thank Robert Woosnam-Savage, Curator of Armour and Edged Weapons at the Royal Armouries, who saw the potential in the Conan Doyle Papers and was instrumental in their acquisition; Peter Day of the Surrey News Service, who carried out much of the initial research at The National Archives in Kew and the Parliamentary Archives at Westminster, and identified many of the key documents; and Donald J. La Rocca, Curator in the Arms and Armor Department at the Metropolitan Museum of Art, who very kindly made available Bashford Dean's archives relating to his mission to Europe in 1917 on behalf of the US Ordnance Department, and his subsequent work on helmets and body armour.

This present work was undertaken as part of the Royal Armouries' First World War Archives Project, which was made possible as a result of a generous grant from the Esmée Fairbairn Collections Fund. A travelling exhibition illustrating Conan Doyle's campaign to save the lives of British Tommies has been funded by the Heritage Lottery Fund.

INTRODUCTION

Arthur Conan Doyle is recognised today as the creator of one of the most enduring characters in English literature, but he was also one of the most prominent and influential figures of the late Victorian and Edwardian age. He was a great patriot, and during the Second Boer War (1899–1902) served as a supplementary medical officer with Langman's Field Hospital throughout the typhoid epidemic in Bloemfontein. He wrote a history of the conflict in South Africa, and was awarded his knighthood in 1902 not for his literary achievements, but for defending Britain's conduct of the war, and rebutting the charges of atrocities committed by British troops.[1] Conan Doyle was also a great campaigner on the political, social and economic issues of the day. He was a regular contributor to the letter pages of the national press, and even stood for Parliament twice, as a Liberal Unionist candidate for Edinburgh Central (1900) and Hawick (1906). Conan Doyle warned against the rise of militarism in Germany, and on the outbreak of war raised a volunteer force of 120

1 Sir Arthur Conan Doyle at his desk in 1923. Arthur Conan Doyle Collection, Lancelyn Green Bequest, Portsmouth City Council.

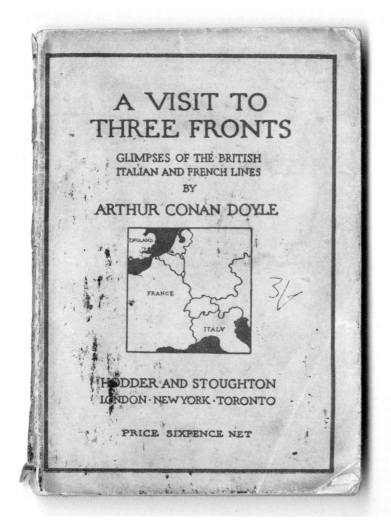

A VISIT TO
THREE FRONTS

GLIMPSES OF THE BRITISH
ITALIAN AND FRENCH LINES
BY
ARTHUR CONAN DOYLE

HODDER AND STOUGHTON
LONDON · NEW YORK · TORONTO

PRICE SIXPENCE NET

2 Conan Doyle's *A Visit to Three Fronts*, published for the War Propaganda Bureau shortly before the Battle of the Somme in 1916. Royal Armouries.

men in his own village, which later became the Crowborough Company in the 6th Royal Sussex Volunteer Regiment, and served as a model for the National Reserve.[2] Then, in September 1914, he (together with a number of other famous authors) was secretly recruited by the War Propaganda Bureau to support the Government's view of the conflict, and to promote Britain's interests at home and abroad. He was not prepared to be a mere puppet, however, and he used his fame to criticise certain aspects of the conduct of the war, in particular the heavy casualties being suffered by British servicemen.

When three cruisers, the *Aboukir*, *Cressy* and *Hogue*, were sunk by a German submarine off the Dutch coast on 22 September 1914 with the loss of nearly 1,500 lives (mostly through drowning), Conan Doyle wrote to the *Daily Mail* criticising the inadequate provision of life-saving equipment on British warships.[3] The Admiralty was reluctant to carry more boats, which might be destroyed or set on fire during an action, and felt that life jackets posed an additional fire risk and would require stowing below deck, making them difficult for men to reach in an emergency. Conan Doyle suggested that sailors should be issued with inflatable rubber lifebelts, and shortly after his letter was published the Admiralty placed an order with David Moseley and Sons of Ardwick, Manchester, for an inflatable swimming collar to be issued to every officer and man in the Royal Navy.[4]

Unfortunately the new swimming collar proved inadequate, and on 1 January 1915 the battleship HMS *Formidable* was torpedoed off Portland Bill with the loss of 35 officers and 512 men from her complement of 780. Conan Doyle was outraged, as he explained in a letter to his friend, John St Loe Strachey, editor of the *Spectator*:

> It is monstrous. The idea that there should be no boats in battleships was started on the supposition that the normal action would be a surface action and that the inflammability of the boats was a danger. The wisdom of this is, I think, open to question, but in these days when we lose a hundred men from submarine explosions to one by gunfire, it really seems beyond argument.[5]

He wrote to the *Daily Mail* again, raising concerns that not enough was being done by the Admiralty to save lives.[6] He criticised the effectiveness of the new swimming collar in rough or ice-cold seas, and suggested that warships should carry collapsible boats, which could be easily stowed and launched when the occasion arose. Conan Doyle confided to Strachey that he doubted whether 'my cry will reach Olympus', but a few days later he received a letter from William Greene, Permanent Secretary to the Admiralty, assuring him that the Lords Commissioners 'have had continuously before them the question of the provision of various forms of life saving apparatus in addition to the swimming collar', and shortly afterwards an order was placed for life jackets and life rafts.[7] However, it was not just the loss of lives at sea that agitated Conan Doyle.

THE FIRST CAMPAIGN, 1915

The British press showed great interest in body armour, shields and other unusual pieces of equipment from the very beginning of the First World War, as well as stories of British servicemen who escaped death or serious injury thanks to books, cigarette cases or watches that deflected shrapnel or bullets. The use of shields was noted as early as August 1914 when they were employed by German infantry during the assault on the Liège forts.[1] This was followed in October by the news that the Russians had used similar devices in the attack on the Polish fortress of Przemysl, and by a Reuters report noting that the French had ordered a large number of shields to be manufactured after successfully testing them in the Argonne.[2] The appearance of the first Canadian troops in Britain aroused much admiration, and a number of newspapers commented on the ingenuity of the MacAdam Shield Shovel with which they were issued.[3] This was an entrenching tool that could also be dug into the ground and used as a shield, and had a hole in the blade through which a rifle could be fired. There was also considerable interest in the small, bullet-proof shields used by German snipers, which were also painted in cubist patterns and futuristic colours in order to facilitate their concealment.[4]

An account of German officers wearing bullet-proof vests on the Eastern Front appeared in September 1914, accompanied by the inevitable jibes about the enemy's lack of courage, but it was not long before enterprising individuals in Britain and France began to develop recognisable forms of body armour.[5] In October the *Birmingham Gazette* reported that Thomas Johnson of Kate's Hill, Dudley, had submitted a vest of mail to the War Office, which he claimed was 'proof against bullet, bayonet and sword thrust', and the special correspondent of the *Morning Post* observed that French troops were wearing bullet-proof protectors made by the citizens of Rheims, which consisted of narrow steel plates sewn inside flannel shirts.[6] The following month it was reported that bullet-proof vests made of two layers of leather with metal plates in between were being advertised in German newspapers, and 'evidently being sold in very large quantities'.[7]

A few days after the war began, the Press Association released the story of a French sergeant who owed his life to a bust of the Kaiser.[8] He had picked up the sculpture as a curiosity in a village school, and stuck it in his haversack. When, shortly afterwards, he was struck in the side by a German bullet, he found that it had glanced off the Kaiser's head, chipping off one of the ends of his moustache. It was not long before similar stories of miraculous escapes began to appear. In September a private in the Royal Scots Fusiliers told a reporter of his remarkable adventure during the advance on Cambria.[9] The fighting had been very severe when he felt the impact of a bullet striking him. Looking down, he discovered that the bullet had gone through his ammunition pouch, struck a clip of cartridges and been deflected away. He was doubly lucky that it had not hit one of the percussion caps in the cartridges, which might have caused it to explode. The following month the King

The GREENWOOD
BULLET DEFLECTOR
:—(PATENTED)—:

TO HELP THE TROOPS.

A Shield for the Soldiers.

Interesting Halifax Invention.

Above we give a sketch of an invention by Ex-Hon. Lieutenant and Quartermaster J. H. T. Greenwood, of Halifax. The idea is to protect the soldier with the rifle. The shield placed on the rifle would not weigh more than a couple of pounds, could be carried on the arm, and would be bullet-proof. It is claimed that it would assist in careful and deliberate shooting, and would greatly minimise the danger to troops in the firing line.

Inner View, Showing
: Sighting Aperture :

It is also claimed that the Shield would be of exceptional value in storming or attacking the enemy's position ; men trained with it would be able to take cover behind it in creeping across the open to attack.

Our soldiers in the trenches being in greater safety behind it would eventually dominate the enemy by the more careful, deliberate, accurate shooting obtained.

Our Snipers would have a far more dangerous weapon and screen for their work ; the shield could be coloured or made to represent the surroundings, and they would thereby be able to enlarge upon their particular usefulness.

J. H. T. GREENWOOD, 28, Union St., Halifax. Tel. 1069.

3 J. H. T. Greenwood's patented Bullet Deflector. Calderdale Museums.

and Queen were visiting a military hospital in London when they spoke to a wounded soldier whose life had been saved by a tin of bully beef.[10] He had been struck by a bullet that had penetrated the tin packed in his haversack, but with insufficient velocity left to carry it through the compressed meat. The tin, with the bullet still embedded in it, was submitted to Their Majesties for inspection, and the toughness of army rations became the subject of innumerable jokes.

This steady stream of stories continued into the early months of 1915, supplemented by descriptions of all manner of novel devices that had begun to appear. E. W. Jackson patented a combined entrenching tool and shield, similar to the MacAdam Shield Shovel, but with a pick-axe at one end and a detachable spade blade at the other, which could be fixed to a soldier's belt and tunic to form a breastplate.[11] J. H. T. Greenwood of Halifax patented a bullet deflector: a cone-shaped shield that could be fitted to a rifle, which would not only 'assist in careful and deliberate shooting' but would also 'minimise the danger to troops in the firing line'.[12] Mawson, Swan and Morgan Ltd of Newcastle produced a bullet-proof mirror, priced 8s. 6d., which could be placed inside a pigskin case, and carried in the breast pocket over the heart.[13] They claimed that it had been successfully tested with a .32-caliber Colt revolver at a range of ten yards. It is unsurprising, therefore, to find the Comptroller General of Patents observing in his annual report that 'applications for darts, mechanical means for throwing bombs and other projectiles, and body armour provide an interesting sidelight on the revival of ancient methods of warfare'.[14] Amongst the inventions in connection with military matters were bullet-proof shields, trench periscopes and sleeping bags, together with combination knives, forks and spoons. *Punch* was even inspired to publish a series of cartoons on such devices, one of which showed the fate of an inventor who offered his bullet-proof cuirass to the War Office.[15]

In April 1915 the Germans launched a new offensive on the Western Front, and by the end of the Second Battle of Ypres a few weeks later the British Army had suffered 65,250 casualties. This was followed by the loss of a further 27,809 men in the Allied counter-offensive in Artois. On 20 July *The Times* published an article in which it noted the growing popularity on the Continent of body armour purchased for private use, and the official employment of large shields by the French and Russians to protect small bodies of infantry as they advanced.[16] It also reviewed the research carried out by Dr Devraigne, recently presented to the Académie nationale de médecine in Paris, which had demonstrated the value of the steel skull cap issued to French troops in reducing the severity of head wounds.[17] The article concluded that:

> The objection to the use of armour has been to a large extent founded upon the fact that it was heavy and difficult to make; but modern conditions of warfare have discounted the question of weight to a great extent. Anyone who has visited our British hospitals knows that head wounds are very frequent indeed. We should certainly reduce the incidence of these wounds if we followed the example of our Allies and gave our men helmets similar to those served out to the French soldiers. We have had eight months in which to consider the question.

Over the next few days a series of follow-up articles and letters from readers were published. An anonymous naval surgeon reviewed the medical evidence; the research into head wounds and the danger of infection carried out by Dr Delorme, Medical Inspector General of the French Army; and the work of Professor Le Dentu and Dr Devraigne investigating the effectiveness of the French helmet.[18] He observed that although the human body was very easy to penetrate, shrapnel often became embedded only an inch or two below the surface of the skin, and the ribs sometimes deflected bullets from the heart and other vital organs. He also noted the numerous instances of 'miraculous escapes due to watches, tobacco tins and pocket books', and concluded that any form of protection would prevent a large number of bullet and shrapnel wounds. He drew attention to the work of his colleague, Dr A. J. Hewitt, who, as a result of treating the wounded on board HMS *Pegasus* after her engagement with the *Königsberg* off Zanzibar, had suggested that 'a coat of light chain-armour or even leather' would be invaluable in protecting officers and men stationed on the bridge, or other exposed positions on-board ship.[19] The anonymous naval surgeon felt that Hewitt's analysis could be applied equally to the situation in the trenches. He concluded that:

> It cannot be too strongly insisted upon that these light wounds are very dangerous because in them, as in the severe wounds, dirt becomes lodged and gangrene and blood-poisoning are hatched. Armour of one kind or another would prevent these light wounds altogether, and so wipe out at a stroke a huge mass of septic cases which are at present filling our hospitals, maiming our soldiers and emptying our exchequer.[20]

Edward Davson, a prominent West India merchant and sugar plantation owner with estates in British Guiana, wrote regarding his own experiments on body armour and helmets.[21] He reported that, with regard to body armour, he had been unable to find a steel plate strong enough to stop a bullet at medium range that would not prove too heavy to wear, and he felt that even if one could be found then the impact from a bullet would be likely to knock a man down. He believed that body armour could be produced to resist shrapnel, but was concerned that bullets, which under other circumstances would pass through the body with little injury, might carry fragments of steel plate into the flesh, thus causing more serious, or even fatal, injuries. He was concerned that the reduction in the number of shrapnel wounds might therefore be balanced by an increase in serious bullet wounds. However, Davson considered that since any bullet penetrating the head would prove fatal, the adoption of a steel helmet capable of providing protection against shrapnel would be effective in reducing the number of head injuries without a corresponding increase in fatal wounds. He had tried to develop a steel helmet that was of sufficient weight to stop shrapnel and light enough to be comfortable to wear, but was forced to admit it had proved beyond his ability and that 'the matter rests with others'.

On 22 July *The Times* reported that the British Army had decided to follow the example of their French allies and adopt a steel helmet.[22] It also revealed (without attributing the authority of its source) that a number of ideas for bullet-proof breastplates had been submitted to the military authorities, but so far none had been found to be practicable. *The Times* observed that to defeat the German Mauser bullet at 80 yards would require a steel plate about $^1/_4$ in thick and weighing $7^1/_4$ lb per square foot and, at between 110 and 120 yards, a steel plate $^1/_4$ in thick and weighing 5 lb per square foot; but even then the impact would be likely to knock a man to the ground. It considered that such a breastplate would be impossible to carry, and doubted whether the steel could be shaped without adversely affecting its resistance. The article noted that a steel plate $^1/_{16}$ in thick would stop shrapnel and spent bullets, but raised concerns that if hit by direct fire, the plate would be perforated and the bullet deformed, with the result that a severe wound would be inflicted.[23]

In a further contribution to the debate, Charles ffoulkes, Curator of the Tower Armouries, examined the decline in the use of body armour since the middle of the 17th century, and concluded that it was due as much to the inability of armourers to produce plate of sufficient quality, and to fashion armour capable of deflecting a sword or bullet, as it was to the thickness and weight of steel required.[24] He suggested that any modern helmet or armour 'must be of the finest tempered steel fashioned in such a way that everywhere a convex surface is presented to the bullet'. ffoulkes felt unable to comment with authority on the argument that the bullet would deform or fragments of plate be carried into the body, and so cause more serious or even fatal wounds, but was inclined to believe that the protection afforded against spent bullets and glancing shots outweighed the risks. He also considered that body armour, well made and with the weight properly distributed, need not add significantly to the burden of the modern soldier, which he calculated at nearly 60 lb, particularly as he believed that much of his existing equipment could be discarded without lessening his fighting efficiency. He dismissed as ineffective French and German attempts to produce a corselet made from small steel plates about 1mm thick and joined together by interlinked rings, and expressed doubts over the design of the new head gear (Casque Adrian modèle 15) adopted by the French. He also raised serious concerns over the effectiveness of the helmets that had begun to appear for sale in London, and wondered whether some form of proof-testing should be adopted, such as the Armourers' Guilds had practised in the past. He concluded his comments by soliciting gifts to the Tower Armouries: 'It would be of great

4 Charles ffoulkes, Curator of the Armouries at the Tower of London. Royal Armouries.

technical interest to show side by side the defences of former times and the modern armour used in the present war.'

Charles ffoulkes's search for inspiration in the past was closely followed by the observations of Maj. Gen. Desmond O'Callaghan, former President of the Ordnance Board, who recalled that, when in charge of the Gun Wharf at Portsmouth, he had invited the then Curator of the Tower Armouries, Viscount Dillon, to identify a number of massive wrought-iron head pieces weighing about 25 or 30 lb each.[25] These proved to be helmets worn by sappers engaged in digging trenches during siege operations, when their heads appearing above the top of the gabion or sap roller were exposed to enemy fire, and had been in common use from the 17th to 19th centuries.

It was only natural that Conan Doyle should participate in the debate, given his professional values as a doctor and his interest in saving lives, but his concern over the casualties being suffered by British soldiers was not entirely impersonal. His wife's brother, Capt. Malcolm Leckie of the Royal Army Medical Corps, had died of wounds on 28 August 1914 during the retreat from Mons, whilst his godson, Lt Arthur Oscar Hornung, attached to the 2nd Battalion, Essex Regiment, had been killed on 6 July 1915 during the Second Battle of Ypres, when the trench in which he was sheltering was hit by an artillery shell. Then, on 28 July 1915, the day after his letter appeared in *The Times*, his brother-in-law, Maj. Leslie William Searles Oldham, 63rd Company, Royal Engineers, was killed by a sniper at Festubert, just a few days after his arrival in France. Conan Doyle believed that:

> Such actions as that of May 9 [the Battle of Aubers Ridge], where several brigades lost nearly half their numbers in endeavouring to rush over the 300 yards which separated us from the German trenches, must make it clear that it is absolutely impossible for unprotected troops to

5 'A strange apparition – Ned Kelly's flight and capture', *Illustrated Australian News*. State Library Victoria.

pass over a zone which is swept by machine guns. Therefore you must either for ever abandon such attacks or you must find artificial protection for the men.[26]

Conan Doyle reminded readers that his own interest in the use of armour dated back to the Boer War, when he had suggested that the development of portable bullet-proof shields would provide the infantry with cover as they advanced over open ground swept by enemy fire.[27] He remembered that the celebrated Australian bushman, Ned Kelly, had used home-made armour to resist arrest from the Victoria Police, and asked: 'If the outlaw could do it, why not the soldier?'. He also recalled the numerous cases where a bullet had become lodged in a Bible, cigarette case or watch and thus saved a man's life, and asked why it was not possible 'to do systematically what has so often been the result of a happy chance'. He was aware of the concerns that fragments of the armour might enter the body and cause more serious injuries, and so suggested that only the most vulnerable parts of the body need be protected: the head with a helmet, and the heart with a curved plate of highly tempered steel. He felt that the severing of a major artery (not a common injury from a rifle bullet) could not be prevented without complete armour, but that wounds to the abdomen, which were no longer fatal thanks to advances in modern surgery, could be protected against by another curved plate. He argued that with these three simple precautions the death rate from rifle and machine gun fire, as well as shrapnel, would be greatly reduced.

Conan Doyle saw body armour as part of a soldier's everyday equipment, but he proposed that, on those occasions where troops were asked to attack a heavily defended position, large shields made of armour plate could be used. He suggested that such shields linked together could provide each company or platoon with complete protection from enemy fire in a manner similar to a Roman *testudo*. They could be mounted on wheels to enable them to be moved more easily over the ground, which would be cleared as far as possible of obstacles in advance, until the troops were close enough to storm the enemy trenches. He saw shields as a special item of equipment that would only be brought up to the front lines when they were needed for an assault.

No sooner had Conan Doyle's letter appeared in *The Times* than it was reprinted in newspapers all over Britain and the Dominions, in particular Australia and New Zealand, whose troops were heavily engaged in Gallipoli. The writer and former All-for-Ireland League MP, Moreton Frewen, responded by drawing attention to the use of a cart-shield invented by General Roy Stone, and used by US infantry during the latter stages of the Cuban War.[28] He recalled that an example had been purchased by staff at the British Embassy in Washington during the Boer War and had been sent to Aldershot to be tested, but did not know what had happened to it thereafter.

A reporter from the *Daily Graphic* sought out the views of Sir Hiram Maxim, the inventor of the machine gun. Maxim expressed doubts as to whether the nature of the terrain would

6 Sir Hiram Maxim, inventor of the machine gun. Royal Armouries.

facilitate the use of mobile shields, but thought that body armour made of nickel steel, although it would have to be as much as $1/4$ in thick to stop a modern projectile at short range, and as a result be very heavy, could be carried by a man easily enough over a short distance.[29] The mining engineer and late Government Inspector of Mines and Explosives in South Africa, Edgar Philip Rathbone, wrote to the *Spectator* claiming to have improved upon the effectiveness of the French corselet.[30] He maintained that his modified design was shrapnel-proof, and that, when struck by a bullet at long range, the metal plates simply bent inwards, causing no more than a scratch to the flesh or a tear to clothing, while at short range they simply disintegrated into a fine dust. Rathbone's idea had little merit, but by remarkable coincidence his son Basil would later go on to play Sherlock Holmes in no fewer than 14 films made between 1939 and 1946.

Conan Doyle's ideas also appeared in the *New York Times* and other newspapers throughout the United States, where he was very popular as a result of his novels and a successful lecture tour before the war.[31] Bashford Dean, the Curator of Armor at the Metropolitan Museum of Art, believed that his suggestions should 'be seriously considered by the British authorities', and wrote a detailed article in which he analysed the entire question of whether troops should wear armour.[32] Dean reviewed the decline in use of armour that had occurred in the 17th century as a consequence of the high cost of the best-quality plate armour, the availability of cheap mass-produced or common heavy armour, and the incomplete protection it offered against fire-arms. He echoed many of the observations of Charles ffoulkes, that armour made of fine steel, curved and highly polished, would deflect modern projectiles. He was aware that if a bullet punctured the plate, it might mushroom and cause more serious wounds, but considered on balance that there would be many more instances of bullets glancing off or failing to penetrate. Nor did he believe that the weight of armour would prove burdensome to the modern soldier if it was well made and evenly distributed.

Dean noted that heavy armour had been made in the past for those engaged in siege warfare, and felt that providing troops with protection to the head, torso, back, groin and thighs would save many lives from shrapnel and spent bullets. He was particularly concerned that the forehead and neck should be properly covered, and recalled the heavy siege helmets of the past – where the weight was borne by the shoulders – and the Cromwellian 'pot', with its pronounced peak and lobster-tail neck-guard. He also noted the successful use of shields by the Japanese during the war with Russia (1904–5). Dean recognised that thorough tests of modern steel would have to be undertaken, but he was convinced that armour could be produced quickly and economically. He believed that a motor vehicle could be readily converted into a travelling armoury to carry such equipment to those parts of the line where they were most needed. He felt that even if it was not possible to provide every soldier with armour, it could be used by pickets, wire-cutters or sharpshooters, and camouflaged to help soldiers blend into their surroundings. He concluded: 'When one considers the value to the community of even one soldier, surely no nation should afford not to protect him as best it can … If armor will save even a few hundreds of men it will certainly pay as a national investment to use it. The time will soon come, I prophesy, when governmental commissions will take up this matter effectively.'

Conan Doyle received a number of letters in response to his ideas. Some were from serving officers who agreed that something was badly needed, whilst others came from private individuals who had invented all manner of devices. These he acknowledged in a second letter to *The Times*.[33] He was particularly impressed with one idea for a mobile shield, which had already been tested in Flanders 'with results which not only satisfied the General of that division, but caused several others to express a strong desire to be supplied with a similar method of shielding an attack from fire, especially machine-gun fire'.[34] He made a summary of the suggestions he received, and sent it to the Inventions Branch at the War Office, but sadly neither this nor the original letters have survived.

At the time that Conan Doyle was sending his ideas on body armour and shields to the War Office, the responsibility for the design, manufacture and supply of munitions was in the process of passing (not without much interdepartmental friction) to the new Ministry of Munitions, which may have delayed a formal response to his letter.[35] It is equally possible that the War Office simply chose to ignore him as *persona non grata*. Conan Doyle had openly criticised the department during the Boer War for failing to respond to his idea for adapting rifles to enable them to deliver high-angle fire against enemy troops sheltering in trenches or behind rocks, and in his history of the conflict he had dared to suggest that the British Army was in need of reform.[36] Conan Doyle was not to be put off, however. He wrote again on 18 November, and this time received a reply from Ernest Moir, Comptroller of the new Munitions Inventions Department (MID), which had been set up to deal with the large number of proposals that were being received by the Ministry of Munitions from outside inventors.[37] Moir was an engineer by profession, and he explained that bullet-proof armour plate of the highest-quality steel was 7 mm thick and weighed about 12 lb per square foot. He therefore calculated that a shield measuring 1 ft 6 in wide by 2 ft 6 in long would weigh approximately 45 lb, and so add significantly to the burden already being carried by the average infantryman. He was not entirely unsympathetic to Conan Doyle's concerns, however, and asked for his views on the usefulness of light, shrapnel-proof body armour, which was then under consideration.

7 Ernest Moir, Comptroller of the Munitions Inventions Department (1915–16). Private collection.

8 Henry Goold-Adams, Comptroller of the Munitions Inventions Department (1916–19). National Portrait Gallery.

Conan Doyle was evidently willing to engage in an exchange of ideas, as he wrote to the MID once more in December. Unfortunately, by this time Moir, who was unpopular with the War Office, had been sent to New York to organise the supply of munitions from the USA. His replacement, Col Henry Goold-Adams of the Royal Artillery, sent a reply that was less than encouraging.[38] He thanked Conan Doyle for his 'interesting letter', but summarily dismissed his suggestions on body armour, stating that:

> while it might be possible for a man to stand up to an occasional bullet, or even several, he certainly could not stand, much less advance under, the fire which would inevitably be directed upon him. Moreover, the armour required to protect a man completely would weigh, according to my calculations, something like 300 lbs., but even supposing that it weighed no more than 200, it is obvious that such a weight would be prohibitive.

Goold-Adams may have been unimpressed with his ideas, but Conan Doyle received welcome support from Dr Caleb Saleeby, a fellow graduate in medicine from Edinburgh University. Saleeby had abandoned his clinical practice in favour of a career as a writer and journalist on public health and social issues. He became a leading proponent of the theory of eugenics, and helped set up the Eugenics Education Society in 1907, although he later came to disagree with some of his fellow members' more radical views. A fervent socialist, he joined the Fabian Society in 1910, and when the *New Statesman* was founded in 1913 he became the science correspondent, although because of Saleeby's eccentricities the editor, Clifford Sharp, asked him to write under the pseudonym 'Lens'. When war broke out Saleeby offered to lecture to new recruits on the importance of military hygiene – in particular the dangers of typhoid fever and venereal disease – but quickly came to realise that soldiers needed to be protected not only from sickness and disease, but also from the weapons of the enemy.[39]

At the beginning of November 1915 photographs appeared in the newspapers showing examples of the new French helmet, which, although dented and perforated, had saved the lives of the soldiers who wore it.[40] Lens was prompted to write an article advocating the protection of the head, heart and other vital organs.[41] He observed that research carried out during the Boer War and the Russo-Japanese War had found that, because of the characteristics of modern ammunition and improvements in surgery, bullets were only likely to kill if they struck certain limited areas of the body. He therefore considered that 'a very limited amount of armour of the right kind, in the right places, might save many lives without seriously, or at all, interfering with the soldier's mobility by reason of its weight'.

Lens believed that, if the military authorities had valued the lives of their troops, they would have carried out experiments after the Boer War, which might have resulted in the development of the steel helmet rather than the adoption of the unpopular Broderick forage cap. He hoped that British soldiers would soon be equipped with effective protection for the head, but raised concerns about both the design of the new helmet, and the quality of the steel being used. He asked whether the War Office had sought expert advice in its development from scientists and physicians, such as J. O. Arnold, Professor of Metallurgy at Sheffield University; Sir Joseph Thompson, winner of the Nobel Prize for Physics; and Sir Victor Horsley, the respected surgeon and neuroscientist. He suggested that tests should be carried out to discover the best kind of steel for the purpose by shooting at helmets placed upon actual human skulls; that the form of the helmet should be designed in relation to the probable angle of impact of the missiles it was intended to counter; and that the type of injuries that resulted to the soft tissue, scalp and skull should be carefully studied.

Although Lens was primarily interested in the development of the steel helmet, he felt that the heart should also be protected. He was uncertain how the chest protectors that he had seen soldiers wearing in the newsreels were constructed (either with overlapping or sutured plates), or if they were effective. He thought, however, that it would

> be very surprising if the experience and inventiveness of our ancestors have not furnished us, in our museums, with types of armour, which could be tested with rifle-bullets and bombs and shrapnel and shell and bayonets, and the best adopted. The experience of the Navy might help also in respect of the precise types of steel most suited for using in the making of the kind of plate, or mail, that is thought best.

Lens was appalled that the question of protecting the troops was only being raised after British losses had reached half a million men, and hoped that the matter would be dealt with 'on the lines of open-minded and intelligent experiment'. He doubted whether the French helmet, or the corselet made of small plates, or the body armour made of flat steel plates on sale in Selfridges, represented the result of any serious research. He realised that soldiers might be wary of such protection, but believed that for the sake of freedom 'they must consent to wear steel as well as wield it'.

Questions regarding the provision of steel helmets were also being asked in Parliament, and Harold Tennant, Under-Secretary of State for War – in response to a request from John Bryce, Liberal MP for the Inverness District of Burghs, and Sir Reginald Neville, Unionist MP for Wigan – had confirmed that after successful trials Sir John French, Commander in Chief of the British Army in France and Flanders, had asked for a large number to be supplied, and that his request was in the process of being fulfilled.[42] Bryce continued to press,

9 Sir Robert Hadfield with His Majesty King George V in 1919. Picture Sheffield.

and asked when the order had been placed, how many had been ordered, and how many had been issued to the troops at the Front.[43] As it happened, the manufacture of the steel helmet (based on a design patented by John Brodie) had begun at the end of September, and quickly reached the rate of 850 per day when the specification was suddenly changed to a steel with a higher manganese content at the suggestion of the renowned metallurgist Sir Robert Hadfield.[44] Unfortunately the new tougher steel was only available from one firm, Thomas Firth and Sons of Sheffield, and being very brittle it proved difficult to stamp. The problems were overcome, but production was delayed as a result. In the Commons, therefore, Tennant declined to give any specific details that might reveal information to the enemy, but stated that thousands of helmets had already been supplied, and it was expected that the Commander in Chief's requirements would be met very shortly. Bryce was far from placated, however, and asked Tennant if he was aware that French troops had been issued with steel helmets more than six months previously.

Nevertheless, the value of the steel helmet had been recognised and action taken, whereas the need for additional protection in the form of body armour and shields had not been proven. The official position was summarised by Tennant in response to a question from Athelstan Rendall, Liberal MP for Thornbury in Gloucestershire, which was clearly inspired by Lens's article. The Under-Secretary of State for War assured Rendall that the proper authorities had been consulted on the design of the new helmet, and that large quantities had already been sent out, but noted that the final scale of supply would ultimately be determined by the Commander in Chief.[45] He also stated that a number of ideas for body armour and shields had been submitted and tested, but the difficulty of devising something that was not too heavy to be carried and would resist penetration had not been solved. He confirmed that tests had been carried out on commercially manufactured body armour, but none of these had proved of practical value.

As 1915 drew to a close Edward Bagnall Poulton, Professor of Zoology at the University of Oxford, delivered the prestigious Romanes Lecture, taking as his theme the need to make more effective use of science in order to achieve victory in the current conflict.[46] Poulton was critical of the 'national neglect of science', which he felt began in public schools with the discouragement of science compared with the classics. He believed that the under-representation of scientists in Parliament and the Government had resulted in the adoption of ill-conceived policies, and cited the example of the Declaration of London, which had failed to declare cotton as contraband and to prohibit the export of linseed oil, both of which were essential constituents in the manufacture of gun-cotton and nitroglycerine. He also observed that scientific studies had shown Germany was unable to produce enough food to

10 Edward Bagnall Poulton, Professor of Zoology, University of Oxford. Private collection.

supply her population, and yet at the beginning of the war the Government had allowed her to import vast quantities of foodstuffs.

Poulton was especially critical of the British Army, who had failed to take advantage of science to adapt to the new conditions of trench warfare. He gave various examples of ideas put forward by scientists that had either been 'pigeon-holed' by the War Office or adopted only after a long delay. Poulton noted that helmets were finally being supplied in large quantities, but that thin armour had been dismissed as dangerous. He suggested that heavy armour could be produced for troops engaged in special duties where rapid movement was not required, such as 'listening posts, patrolling for enemy snipers, superintending wire, trench work etc'. He recalled that the late Revd F. Jervoise Smith, Lecturer in Engineering, had conducted a number of experiments with bullet-proof shields, which had shown encouraging results, and had offered to disclose the principles of his method to the authorities. Poulton concluded his attack on the Army by criticising the failure to find a better use for 'the flower of our youth, in intellect as in every other quality'. He had good cause. A number of his students had volunteered at the beginning of the war, with tragic results, and his own son, Lt Ronald William Poulton Palmer, 4th Battalion, Royal Berkshire Regiment, formerly of Balliol College, Oxford and captain of the England Rugby XV, had been killed by a sniper while superintending repair work in the trenches in front of Ploegsteert Wood in Flanders on 5 May 1915.

In actual fact, the authorities had not been as idle as was imagined. As early as December 1914 Lt Col Maurice Hankey, Secretary to the War Council, concerned at the growing impasse on the Western Front, had written a memorandum in which he noted that in the past all kinds of devices had been used to attack heavily defended positions.[47] Hankey wondered if the provision of special equipment might help overcome the present impasse, and asked if modern science could do more to help. He even went so far as to suggest the development of a number of devices: heavy steam rollers fitted with machine guns to flatten barbed wire and provide cover to the infantry; bullet-proof shields or armour to protect soldiers; smoke bombs to be thrown toward the enemy's trenches to screen advancing troops; rockets fitted with grappling hooks and rope to clear wire entanglements; and spring catapults or pumping apparatus to throw bombs or burning petrol into the enemy's trenches.

A few days later Winston Churchill, First Lord of the Admiralty, wrote to the Prime Minister to add his support to Hankey's memorandum.[48] Churchill believed that it would be relatively easy to fit a number of steam tractors with small armoured shelters that could be used to accommodate men and machine guns, and caterpillar tracks to enable them to cross the battlefield with ease. He felt that smoke projectors could be developed that would release a dense black smoke to screen an attack and deceive the enemy. He also believed that the provision of some form of protection for the troops by means of shields, 'some to carry, some to wear, some to wheel', was another obvious experiment that should be conducted. He even revealed that he had already given instructions for 20 mobile shields, based on the best design that could be devised, to be produced for testing. As a result of Churchill's interest, the early development of shields was actually undertaken by the Royal Naval Air Service (RNAS) at Wormwood Scrubs. A number of examples were then sent to the British Expeditionary Force in France and Flanders.

In March 1915, the Army Council wrote to General Head Quarters (GHQ) in France, noting that a considerable number of bullet-proof breastplates of various sizes and weights were being submitted to the War Office by inventors. Most of these, it was argued, offered limited protection against frontal fire only, and the Council asked the Commander in Chief for his opinion on the utility of such devices for men engaged in particularly dangerous duties.[49] GHQ responded by requesting that experiments be carried out, and specified that the weight of such portable shields should not exceed 25 lb, that they should be curved back to take the shape of the body, and that it would be advantageous if they were combined with a loophole. GHQ added the proviso, however, that such devices should only be used by scouts, and not by formed bodies of troops. A design for a portable shield was quickly produced, but the War Office had barely begun their experiments when the Ministry of Munitions was established to take over responsibility for the design, manufacture and supply of munitions.[50]

In August 1915 (shortly after the conclusion of the debate in *The Times* and Conan Doyle's letter to the Inventions Branch) David Lloyd George, the new Minister of Munitions, asked Ernest Moir at the MID for information on the potential use of shields. Moir submitted a preliminary report on 13 August, in which he noted that, in addition to existing patents for such devices, approximately 50 proposals for bullet-proof shields had been received since the outbreak of the war.[51] He provided illustrations of some of the different ideas, including shields combined with entrenching tools, portable shields to be carried or worn, and mobile shields mounted on wheels. He drew particular attention to a mobile shield designed by Lt Cyril Aldin Smith of the Royal Naval Armoured Car Service that had already been tried at the Front. Its use on good ground (roads and other hard surfaces) had been commented upon favourably by senior officers. He also noted that another mobile shield devised by Maj. Thomas G. Hetherington and Lt Kenneth P. Symes of the RNAS, which was propelled on the endless track (or pedrail) system rather than wheels, was reported to have overcome the problem of moving over soft or rough ground. It measured 15 ft long by 4 ft 6 in high, had a crew of 12 men, and was capable of protecting 35 to 40 men, but the armour plate required to resist rifle and machine gun at close range made it very heavy

11 David Lloyd George, Minister of Munitions (1915–16), Secretary of State for War (1916) and Prime Minister (1916–22). Private collection.

(it weighed over one-and-a-half tons) and slow. Moir felt that 'Without having consulted the Military Authorities I cannot express any opinion as to the fighting value of portable armoured shields, but I imagine they might be of considerable use in advancing machine guns, bombing parties and wire cutting parties in the face of rifle or machine gun fire.'

Moir submitted a second report on 19 August based on information he had received from Maj. Richard Oakes, the Inspector of Iron Structures at the Department of Fortifications and Works.[52] He began by providing an update on the new patterns of loopholed shields (for use in the trenches) and sap shields (to protect soldiers engaged in constructing field works) that had been developed since the beginning of the war, and reported that an order for 20 experimental machine gun loopholed plates had recently been placed. Moir observed that body armour had been used for many years, most notably during the American Civil War, but considered the increased penetrative power of modern rifle and machine gun ammunition made its adoption in the current conflict more difficult. Oakes's department was not concerned with the development of body shields, but he supported the view of Sir Douglas Haig, Commander of the First Army in France, who believed that 'a satisfactory bullet-proof shield which can be worn and carried by the soldier has not yet been produced, and it is doubtful if such a shield can be made within a practicable weight'. Moir estimated that even a small shield, which measured 10–12 in wide by 15–18 in long, and offered only partial protection to the body, would weigh between $20\frac{1}{2}$ and 24 lb, and felt that it was for the military authorities to decide if the extra burden was worthwhile.

Moir also reviewed various attempts that had been made to design mobile shields. He noted that 200 shields based on a sketch by Brigadier General Louis C. Jackson, Assistant Director of Fortifications and Works, had been sent to France for trials. They were 6 ft long by 2 ft wide, mounted on two wheels, and were designed to protect one man. These had been rejected by GHQ, however, as they were very heavy, awkward to lift up and launch from the front-line trenches, and difficult to move over rough terrain. In addition, owing to the nature of their movement over uneven ground, they neither afforded any great measure

12 The mobile shield designed by Lt Cyril Aldin Smith, RNAS. Parliamentary Archives, Lloyd George Papers.

of protection nor provided any cover from flanking fire. Moir observed that a number of large shields capable of protecting between four and ten men had been developed by the RNAS, but these had also been rejected by the Chief Engineer at GHQ and not even sent to the front lines. Moir noted that the War Office was currently in the process of developing a three-wheeled design, but was equally pessimistic about its use. He felt that wheeled shields might be useful for advancing along roads, or across hard ground, or for attacking in towns, and the successful development of the pedrail system might provide a solution to the difficulty of moving over rough ground. He noted, however, that it currently appeared impossible to develop a mobile shield weighing less than between 20 and 24 lb per super foot, and expressed the view that to develop a shield able to carry any sort of gun, or to provide protection for a large number of men, 'one is driven to think that a mechanically propelled armoured vehicle, contrived to pass over any kind of rough ground, wire entanglements, or any such obstructions will form the only possible type of bullet-proof mobile shield. The experiments now being carried out with the Caterpillar or end-less track, if successful, may be the solution.'

Moir recognised that the use of shields appealed to those who were not familiar with the difficulties of manoeuvring them over uneven ground, through barbed wire and over other obstructions, and promised the Minister that his department would look again at the problem. He was forced to admit, however, that an efficient design 'to protect the advance against the enemies' trenches of large numbers of men and guns across the bullet-swept zone which intervenes between the opposing forces' seemed a remote possibility. Two months later Moir reported to Lloyd George that the MID had completed drawings for a new mobile shield based on the designs of Lieutenants Smith and Symes, and that a quote had been received for manufacturing an example to test.[53]

Lloyd George asked Moir if some of the breastplates then being sold by the Junior Army and Navy Stores could be tested to see if they were of any potential use.[54] Experiments were quickly carried out with a .22 rifle and a saloon pistol fired at a range of 10 ft on a waistcoat composed of small steel plates connected by rings and riveted to the fabric (the Franco-British cuirass); a chest shield consisting of four large plates covered with khaki drill and protected at the joints by narrow metal strips (the Dayfield Body Shield); and a steel cap designed to fit inside a service cap (similar to the French skull cap); but only the latter resisted attempts to puncture it.[55] Further tests with a .45 Colt automatic pistol at a range of 25 yards confirmed these results, although the steel cap was destroyed when the welds holding the pieces together gave way.[56] In his covering letter Moir concluded that the articles examined not only failed to provide protection, but also that they risked additional injuries caused by the deformation of the bullet, by damage to the protective material itself and by pieces of the armour being driven into the body.[57]

The subject remained high on Lloyd George's agenda, and on 29 November (two days after Lens's article in the New Statesman) 'armoured protection for men' appeared on a list of items that he wished to discuss at a meeting with Maj. Gen. John Philip Du Cane, who had recently been appointed Director General of the Munitions Design Department.[58] The discussions appear to have had some effect, as on 16 December (two days after his letter to Conan Doyle) Goold-Adams reported to the Minister that a sub-committee had been set up consisting of members of the Munitions Inventions Department, the Munitions Design Department, the Trench Warfare Supply Department and the Royal Army Medical Corps to look further into the question of body armour.[59] It marked a significant breakthrough.

In December 1915 the War Office wrote to GHQ once more expressing its concerns over the number of ideas for shields being submitted by inventors, as well as its apprehension about advertisements inviting the public to buy shields of doubtful quality to send to the troops.[60] It asked for a definite decision to be made on the provision of body armour. Further, it noted that tests with portable shields had failed to overcome the problem of weight, and enquired if a body shield made of 1 mm steel and proof against shrapnel bullets and splinters should be provided. Sir Douglas Haig, who had recently succeeded Sir John French as Commander in Chief of the British Army in the Field, held to his view that the provision of bullet-proof body armour was not practicable given the weight, but noted that there was a demand for a portable shield that would resist enemy bullets at close range, and that 'some form of light protection for the body against shell splinters and grenade fragments would be valuable for men taking part in trench warfare'.[61] He added three general conditions that such a light body shield should fulfil: it must afford all-round protection; it must not interfere with the free use of both arms or impede the movements of the wearer; and it must not be too heavy so as to tire men engaged in duties of a prolonged and arduous nature (such as throwing grenades). He even went so far as to suggest that a leather jerkin covered with small metal plates might be suitable. A fourth condition, that the body shield should not exceed a weight of 15 lb, was evidently added at a later date.

Lloyd George continued to press the MID, stating that he was 'very anxious in the prospects of securing an adequate body-shield which would at any rate reduce by a material percentage the casualties from rifles, machine guns and shells', and forwarding a copy of an advertisement for the Dayfield Body Shield that he had seen in one of the newspapers.[62]

13 Sir Douglas Haig, Commander in Chief of the British Armies in France and Flanders (1915–18). Library of Congress.

Goold-Adams advised the Minister that the sub-committee on body armour had already met with the result that some preliminary tests had been carried out.[63] Although he felt that the weight of armour required to resist rifle and machine gun bullets was prohibitive, and no defence seemed achievable against high-explosive shells, he thought that it might be possible to produce light body armour from the same steel as the new helmet. He reported that tests were about to be made to find a suitable material for body armour along the lines requested by GHQ, and that the Army Medical Department were collating statistics on wounds to ensure that any design would produce the maximum protection.[64] Goold-Adams also informed Lloyd George that a Dayfield Body Shield made in 18-gauge steel had been tested, and although it had proved effective against shrapnel bullets it had given poor results against bomb fragments. The manufacturers had then provided a shield made of 16-gauge steel, which gave good results against both, but this was significantly heavier, and so only part of the wearer's body could be protected. He advised the Minister that additional samples of shields made of 16-gauge and 18-gauge steel had been prepared for further tests.

Within a few weeks of Haig's request having been received, the Ministry of Munitions sent a progress report to the Secretary at the War Office, which notified him that 1,000 body shields (the heavy model of Dayfield Body Shield) had been ordered. This appeared to meet two of the three conditions laid down by GHQ.[65] It also noted that recent tests of a protective garment or apron had produced satisfactory results against grenade fragments, and that a final design was now being prepared. This was followed by a second progress report on mobile shields, which informed the War Office that investigations had revealed that a number of shields made by Vickers and Beardmore had been sent to France and Gallipoli, and only two examples remained in Britain (one at the RNAS at Wormwood Scrubs, and the other (a pedrail design) at the Experimental Grounds at Wembley), both of which had been tested on previous occasions.[66] It observed that there were a number of other examples designed by Lt Smith already with the 6th Division in France, and concluded by offering to produce some new designs if required.

A Conan Doyle's 'The Battle of the Somme': part of his history of the British campaign in France and Flanders. *Strand Magazine* 55.329 (May 1918). Adrian Harrington Rare Books.

B Mark I Helmet (Brodie's patent). Royal Armouries.

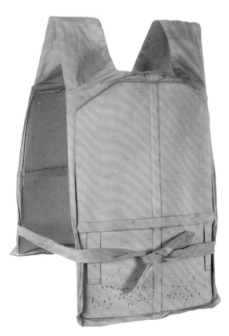

C Dayfield Body Shield (original model). Imperial War Museum, EQU 436.

D Chemico Body Shield. Media Image Photography.

E EOB Body Shield. Imperial War Museum, EQU 236.

F Bomber's Necklet. Imperial War Museum, EQU 3895.

THE SECOND CAMPAIGN, 1916–17

The steel helmet created a considerable stir in the press when it finally began to appear, and although the delays in production meant that only 300,000 had been delivered by the middle of March 1916 the special correspondent of the *Daily Express* was able to report that the 'soup-plates', as the British soldiers had nicknamed them, had saved many lives in the fighting around the Ypres Salient.[1] Saleeby gave his own endorsement to the new helmet in a public lecture at His Majesty's Theatre on Haymarket, and a few days later Lens reviewed its successful development in more detail.[2] He noted that although the censor had prevented the publication of some of his earlier observations on the subject, an effective design had finally been produced after his intervention in November 1915, in which he had called upon the authorities to consult the appropriate experts. He had been permitted to examine a number of helmets submitted for trial at the Ministry of Munitions, all of which were 'perforated and splintered', and was in no doubt that as a result of the extensive tests 'our men are being provided with what is undoubtedly the finest helmet ever made'. He acknowledged that it was heavy, but only manganese steel had proved suitable for the purpose; he was aware that the design was a 'most un-becoming form', but it was

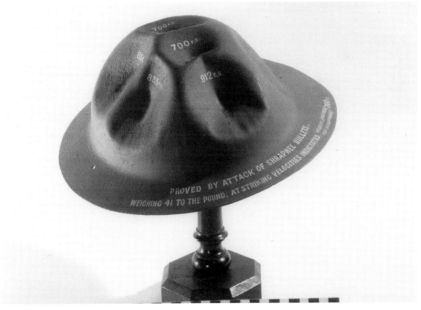

14 The steel helmet designed by John Brodie showing the effects of tests against shrapnel bullets. Royal Armouries. Collection unknown.

effective in deflecting bullets; and he believed that the lining offered good protection to the scalp and the skull in the event that the helmet be perforated.

On 1 July 1916 the British Army launched a major offensive on the Somme to relieve pressure on their French allies, who were engaged in a fierce battle of attrition for Verdun. The majority of the troops that took part in the attack were volunteers, ordinary men from all walks of life, who were enthusiastic but inexperienced and poorly trained. They advanced into battle in long, closely formed lines – a perfect target for German artillery and machine guns – and 57,470 men were lost on the first day. As the scale of the casualties became apparent, Poulton wrote in despair to *The Times*: 'After about a year and a half our military advisers thought it worth while to provide the soldiers with adequate helmets. From all sides we hear of the lives saved by this wonderful ingenuity and resource. After an equal interval we may perhaps hope for some body defence against the hail of machine-gun bullets in No Man's Land.'[3]

Poulton's letter served to reinvigorate the debate. Edward J. Formby observed that France had led the way with the development of helmets, and hoped Britain would do the same with body armour. He noted the widespread sale of commercially manufactured examples, whose advertisements were often accompanied by letters from soldiers testifying to their life-saving capabilities, and wondered why the Government did not supply them to the troops.[4] The publisher and Director of the Rubber Estate Agency, William Frederick de Bois Maclaren, thought it unfair of newspaper correspondents like Poulton to accuse Government departments of inactivity, and, by inference, the staff at the War Office of slacking and 'gross neglect', when they were unable to respond.[5] He recognised that steel helmets had been successful in providing protection from shrapnel, but observed that body armour was another thing entirely. He observed that flat steel plates gave no protection from rifle or machine gun fire, and were the cause of 'ghastly wounds instead of clean perforations'. Maclaren had personally conducted experiments with two $^3/_4$ in steel plates, bound back-to-back with four layers of $^1/_4$ in rubber, but had been unable to prevent rifle bullets from penetrating them 'like paper' at a range of 150 yards. He felt that only heavy steel plates would give the required protection, but that these would be difficult to carry. He felt sure that the War Office was well aware of these facts.

Up until this point serving soldiers had refrained from taking part openly in the discussion, but one who signed himself as 'Wounded in the Push' wrote to express his concern that 'the agitation for body armour … is the work of well-meaning people entirely unacquainted with modern war conditions'.[6] He pointed out that an infantryman already carried between 56 and 63 lb of equipment, and that the addition of body armour weighing a further 4–8 lb would result in a 30 per cent decrease in his efficiency and a 400 per cent increase in his discomfort. 'Wounded in the Push' maintained that the majority of wounds were caused by machine gun fire, and that at close range the bullet made a clean wound, as he could personally testify. He agreed with Maclaren's view that 'by placing an inadequate shield between the bullet and its victim, we simply get a very much worse wound'.

Another serving soldier, writing under the pseudonym 'In Action', was in complete accord.[7] He reminded readers that the steel helmet was not intended to give protection against machine gun or rifle fire, and pointed out the difference between shrapnel bullets, which were soft, spherical projectiles of relatively low velocity, and rifle bullets, which were steel-jacketed, pointed and high velocity. He observed that a shield was only of use against frontal fire and was useless against enfilade fire, and felt that nothing less than body armour made of $^1/_4$ in steel would be useful to protect the heart or abdomen, but that its weight, which he estimated at 15 lb, would hamper the movements of an infantryman already overloaded with weapons and equipment. 'In Action' also raised serious concerns about privately manufactured body armour: 'I might perhaps mention my experience with a body shield which was sent me from home. I was very sceptical about its worth, so took it outside and fired at it with my pistol at 50 yards. The ordinary lead Service bullets went clean through it, carrying jagged splinters with them.'

Poulton remained dubious that the War Office was not guilty of negligence, given that it had taken a year-and-a-half to introduce the steel helmet, and that any serious research on body armour had been carried out:[8] this despite the fact that a similar debate during the Boer War had concluded that a steel plate covering the heart and abdomen would succeed in preventing nearly all fatal wounds, and that even if it could not stop a bullet at short range, it could be shaped in such a fashion as to deflect it. He thought that if a number of men, designated as special machine gun fighters, were stripped of all unnecessary equipment and given body armour for protection, then they could go out and either attack the enemy's machine gun positions themselves, or call upon quick-firing guns (pom-poms) that had been brought up to close range under a smoke screen, or heavy artillery, for support. Poulton recalled that he had offered to reveal to the War Office the principles behind the Revd F. Jervais Smith's experiments with bullet-proof shields, but that they had failed to respond. He also remembered having seen a demonstration of a portable shield designed by Professor Miles Walker at the British Association in Manchester the previous year, and felt that 'surely such methods are worth trying'.[9]

At the end of July the matter was raised once more in the House of Commons, and the Financial Secretary to the War Office, Henry Forster, confirmed in a written answer to Lewis Haslam, Liberal MP for the Monmouth Boroughs, that the question of providing body armour to the troops was awaiting a report from the Commander in Chief.[10] This encouraging sign was followed a few days later by the personal intervention of Lloyd George, the new Secretary of State for War, who in reply to a speech by Winston Churchill declared:

> This idea of protective shields, whether for the head or any other part of the body, I believe, will be developed very considerably. Up to the present no Army has thought fit to utilise it. It has been tried by most Armies, but not very successfully. I believe that we shall, in this respect, as in respect of the helmets, revert to the old methods of warfare when protection of the body was not regarded in the least as detracting from the valour of the men who wore it.[11]

If Conan Doyle had been waiting for an opportunity to rejoin the debate it had now arrived. He had been permitted to travel to France and Flanders earlier in the year as part of his work for the War Propaganda Bureau, to visit GHQ and the troops in the front lines, and to learn about trench warfare for himself.[12] Haig had arranged for him to meet his eldest son, Lt Arthur Alleyne Kingsley Doyle, 1st Battalion, Hampshire Regiment, and he was well aware that a major operation was in the offing. On 1 July the Hampshires had attacked the German positions to the north of Beaumont Hamel, and had lost 11 officers and 310 men killed or missing, and 15 officers and 250 men wounded, including Conan Doyle's son, who was badly injured in the neck by shrapnel.[13]

Conan Doyle maintained that the heavy casualties suffered on the first day of the Battle of the Somme had been caused principally by machine gun fire and not by high explosives, and the tactical problem (as he saw it) was to protect the infantry as they advanced across the narrow gap from their own lines to the German trenches.[14] He revived his idea of using large shields to protect troops when storming heavily defended positions. He was certain that a shield fashioned like that of a Roman soldier, made from $^7/_{16}$ in steel and measuring

15 Lt Arthur Alleyne Kingsley Doyle, 1st Battalion, Hampshire Regiment. Leeds City Council.

3 ft long by 2 ft wide, would stop a bullet fired at point-blank range. He recognised that such shields would be heavy (he estimated the weight at well over 30 lb) but noted that they would not have to be carried very far. He suggested that they be issued to troops in the first wave, who would otherwise be armed solely with grenades, which they would use to destroy the enemy's machine gun positions; the soldiers in the second wave would be armed with rifles, which they would use to occupy and secure the trenches. Conan Doyle believed that shields were a better option than body armour, since they could be turned in any direction, or used to form a screen for a sniper or a wounded man. He was aware of the large number of commercially manufactured body armours, but was not convinced of their effectiveness, despite the large number of letters from men claiming that they had saved their lives. He also recognised the dilemma facing those officers who could afford to buy such items, but might be reluctant to use protection that their men did not possess. Conan Doyle was beginning to lose patience with the inactivity of the authorities. He asked that 'the experiment be made of arming a whole battalion with proper ones [body armour] – and, above all, let it be done at once. Then at last the attack will be on a level with the defence.'

Poulton was delighted with Conan Doyle's intervention, but elsewhere his ideas did not go unchallenged.[15] W. E. Woodward, a metallurgist from the Wilden Ironworks near Stourport, wrote to point out that a shield of the size envisaged would weigh considerably more than estimated (probably around 100 lb) and doubted whether a soldier could advance, let alone run, when encumbered by such additional weight.[16] Lieutenant Colonel F. W. M. Newell, from the Special Hospital for Officers in Kensington, also felt that Conan Doyle had underestimated the weight of such shields. He highlighted the logistical problems of transporting them to the battlefield, and asked how they would be moved up to the front line when required.[17]

Conan Doyle replied immediately, citing the opinion of an experienced soldier, who in the course of numerous discussions had 'never once met an officer who did not think some attempt should be made to produce shields'. He felt that even a crude plate slung from a man's neck would be better than nothing, and pointed out that a solution to the problem would contribute not only to the saving of lives but also to the winning of battles. He acknowledged that he might have underestimated the weight, but felt a heavy shield would have the advantage of absorbing the shock of a bullet's impact. He believed that a shield could be produced using a steel alloy, which might be slightly smaller, but would still protect the vital parts of the body, and be light enough (perhaps only 80 lb) for a man to carry if he was not encumbered with other equipment.[18] He was sure that shields could be transported to the front in motorised transport in the same way as heavy shells. Conan Doyle maintained that if the same effort had been shown in the development of body armour as in 'poison-helmets' (gas masks) then the question would have been settled. He felt that 'the essential thing now is to get to the end of the talk and to actually do something to enable our men to face the machine guns'.

A few days later Conan Doyle returned to the subject in a more detailed article for the *Observer*, in which he argued that the unusual circumstances brought about by trench warfare had removed the main objections to the use of body armour, the weight and the need for soldiers to be able to move rapidly having ceased to matter as the success of an advance was measured in a few hundred yards a day, a few miles being regarded as a major victory.[19] He maintained that the situation on the Western Front was so static that body armour could be brought up to the front-line trenches and left there for the occupants to use just like any other piece of trench equipment. He believed that the German Army was now firmly on the defensive, and as the Allies assumed the offensive only two things would prevent further heavy losses: 'one is the big gun, by which we crush them from a distance; the other is some protective device by which we can bring ourselves unhurt through their shrapnel and machine gun fire'.

Conan Doyle claimed to have received information from 'an experienced observer' who was present at the Battle of the Somme, which showed that the casualties were due to heavy shells (10 per cent), shrapnel (40 per cent), machine guns (45 per cent), and rifles (5 per cent), and on this basis he calculated that 90 per cent of the losses suffered were potentially avoidable.[20] He pointed out that the adoption of the steel helmet had already significantly reduced instances of head wounds from shrapnel, and believed that body armour, either in the form of a large heavy plate covering the body from the neck to the thigh, or a smaller plate covering just the heart, would have a similar impact in minimising casualties from rifle and machine gun fire. He further developed his ideas about infantry attacking heavily defended positions, and argued that the assault troops should be equipped with body armour (not shields) and armed with grenades and automatic pistols, which they would use to suppress the enemy's fire, the follow-up wave being armed with rifles to capture the trench. Conan Doyle could not understand the continued delay: 'The thing can be done … the thing has to be done … surely at last something will now be done.'

Conan Doyle's apparent conversion to the use of body armour may have been as a consequence of the letters he received from Woodward, Newell and others casting doubt on the utility of shields, or the result of a secret meeting with Maj. Albert Stern, Chairman of the Tank Supply Committee. In his book on the development of the tank published shortly after the war, Stern revealed that at this time he was instructed by the Minister of Munitions,

16 Mark IV tank. Royal Armouries.

Edwin Montagu, 'to show him that we were doing something still better to protect the infantry by mechanical means'.[21] He recalled that Conan Doyle was very interested, and that afterwards he kept in close touch with him. Stern does not give the date of the meeting, and Conan Doyle does not mention it in his own memoirs, but it was clearly after the publication of his letters in *The Times* and before tanks made their first appearance on the battlefield at Flers–Courcelette on 15 September 1916. The knowledge that tanks were in production may have led him to concentrate his arguments on the development of body armour.

Lord Sydenham, a former colonial administrator, who had originally served in the Royal Engineers and was an acknowledged expert on fortifications, was less impressed with Conan Doyle's ideas. He believed that the thickness and weight of armour plate sufficient to stop a rifle or machine gun bullet at short ranges made body armour impracticable.[22] He further considered that 'rendering the heart immune would be of no military purpose', as the wounds caused by the reversed bullets of the Germans and the explosive bullets of the Austrians striking other parts of the body were no less fatal. Conan Doyle responded by asking if the preservation of lives was not a military advantage, as it would enable the troops to capture their objective with sufficient strength to retain it in the face of a counter-attack. He continued to argue that body armour would save lives, and cited the recent experience of a sergeant as narrated to him:

> As we turned the corner we saw a German lying round the end of a wall. He had got a machine gun. He turned this damned thing on me and got me on the foot. It didn't stop, but as I was getting near him I felt two kicks over the heart. I didn't wait to see what had happened but bayoneted him. I sat down to see what was the damage. My foot was pretty bad, but when I looked at my left-hand breast pocket I saw two holes in it. I opened my pocket and found that the two

17 George Clarke Sydenham, Baron Sydenham of Combe, former Governor of Victoria. State Library Victoria.

bullets had gone through my metal shaving mirror, my pocket case, and had nosed their way into a book I was carrying.[23]

As the Battle of the Somme continued to rage, with further losses daily announced in the newspapers for minimal gains in territory, Conan Doyle's letters sparked further interest in the British press, as well as in Canada, Australia and New Zealand. His ideas received far more support than criticism. An unknown correspondent in the *Western Daily Press* recalled some experiments conducted on the Continent and in England over 20 years previously (by an Austrian named Scarneo and a German called Dowe) with body armour made from a fibrous material that it was claimed could stop a rifle bullet, and wondered what had become of them.[24] George Lynch developed a large canvas mat filled with a chemically treated cotton wool that was 'practically impenetrable by bayonet and bullet'. It could be used to protect the troops as they advanced across No Man's Land, and then thrown on top of the barbed wire entanglements in front of the enemy's trenches.[25] Demetrius Boulger designed a large steel shield, which protected two men standing, and provided partial cover for others lying down. It had straps to enable it to be carried; struts to support it at an angle of 30 degrees to deflect bullets, and was fitted with a central loophole for a machine gun and others for rifles.[26] Amidst all this enthusiasm there were still those who sounded a note of caution, and the *Dundee People's Journal* published a cartoon entitled 'Hah Wull has a try at inventing', which showed the would-be inventor taking to his heels rather than personally demonstrate the effectiveness of his bullet-proof breastplate in front of a squad of riflemen.[27]

The newspapers also continued to recount stories of miraculous escapes. On 28 July the *Daily Mirror* reported the story of Capt. Hugh Cowell Kinred, 14th Battalion, Gloucester Regiment, who dived on top of a grenade that had landed near seven sleeping men.[28] He was blown onto the top of the parapet of the trench, but apart from his uniform, which

18 Surviving fragment of Capt. Hugh Kinred's Dayfield Body Shield, displayed with the front page of the *Daily Mirror*. Royal Armouries.

was cut to shreds, and a few scratches and bruises, he was unhurt, thanks to the Dayfield Body Shield he was wearing. Kinred received the Military Cross for conspicuous gallantry, and a few weeks later photographs of his tunic and body armour, together with his own modest account of the incident, were published on the front pages of the *Daily Mirror* and the *Daily Express*.[29] In September Pte F. C. Shuter, 10th Battalion, Royal Fusiliers, wrote home to describe how he had escaped serious injury when a bullet had become embedded in his cigarette case. The case became his most cherished item, and pictures showing the bullet still lodged in it were printed in the *Daily Mirror*, where they appeared alongside the advert for the Dayfield Body Shield illustrated with the photographs of Kinred's body armour.[30] In November a Mr Rhodes of Shipley wrote to his local newspaper to say he had received a letter from his son, Pte Harry Rhodes of the Duke of Wellington's Regiment, informing him that in the heavy fighting on the Somme his Chemico Body Shield had saved his life on several occasions, and was now covered in bullet and shrapnel holes.[31]

Once again Conan Doyle received a large number of letters from private individuals who shared his concerns, many of whom had their own ideas for body armour and shields. Miles Walker, Professor of Electrical Engineering at the Municipal School of Technology in Manchester, brought to Conan Doyle's attention his idea for a portable shield, and included photographs of the tests he had conducted at Heaton Park, Buxton, in the previous year with the aid of the Royal Engineers (Figure 19).[32] He had later demonstrated the shield to Maj. Richard Oakes, the Inspector of Iron Structures at the Department of Fortifications and Works, with the help of the 90th Brigade, but his ideas had been rejected. When his attempts to persuade the Ministry of Munitions to conduct trials with his shields failed, he wrote to *The Times* on the subject, only for his letter to be 'struck out by the censor' because it revealed information on experiments with military equipment. Walker was undeterred, however, and told Conan Doyle that he had appealed to a number of MPs in the hope that they would bring pressure to bear on the Government to look into his ideas. George Wakeman of Sparkhill in Birmingham sent Conan Doyle not only a detailed design for armour – consisting of a helmet; breastplate; backplate; and abdomen, arm and leg defences – which he described as 'simple, light, effective & cheap', but also a sketch of a projectile for destroying barbed wire (Figure 20).[33] Wakeman admitted that his suggestions 'did not take root in the official mind', but noted that a sergeant in the trenches had 'heartily approved' of his ideas for armour, and an experienced gunner had commented favourably on his suggestions for a wire entanglement destroyer.

It was not just in Britain where attempts to reduce the casualties being suffered on the Western Front were being frustrated. Arthur Rotsaert, a 2nd Lieutenant in the Royal Belgian Engineers, wrote to Conan Doyle claiming that he had 'made a type of shield giving full and effective protection against the German rifle bullet and shrapnel splinters to the chest and abdomen of the soldiers when they are marching upright and covering them completely when lying flat'.[34] Rotsaert's armour was made of 7 mm steel and weighed just less than 17 lb, but he believed that it might be made in 5.5 mm steel with a corresponding reduction in weight, and still provide protection at a distance of 60 m. The Belgian Board of Inventions had spurned his ideas, declaring that his armour was too heavy, but he remained convinced that the special circumstances of trench warfare made this criticism irrelevant. He argued that armour need only be carried during an assault, and that if the troops had to march any great distance they could simply leave it behind to be picked up by the rear echelons. He offered to send his armour to Conan Doyle, but asked him not to publicise his name or rank in the Belgian Army as this might lead to trouble.

19 Professor Miles Walker's design for a portable shield. Royal Armouries, Conan Doyle Papers.

Mlle Marthe Durand from Paris had also read Conan Doyle's letter in *The Times*, and contacted him regarding the bullet-proof body armour she had developed that had saved the lives of two members of her family, one of whom had been hit in the chest, and the other near the heart.[35] The armour weighed only 3 kg (6 lb 10 oz), but although she had sent samples to the French Army she had not yet received a response. She thought that:

> if it could be tested on the English front, a decision might be more quickly forthcoming. Time is of the essence; there are so many dead to lament already. I am French, and I wish with all my heart that my invention could be useful to all the allied forces. If you so wish, Dear Sir, I will send you a specimen of my bullet-proof armour and with your influence you could persuade the British army to try it out for the well-being of all our dear soldiers.

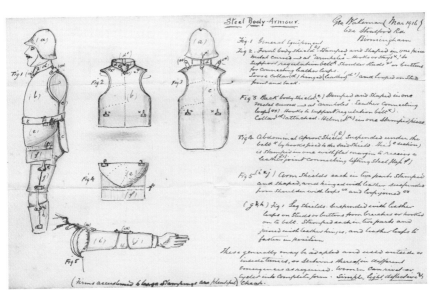

20 George Wakeman's design for body armour. Royal Armouries, Conan Doyle Papers.

Conan Doyle also received letters from a number of commercial manufacturers of body armour. John Pullman, the retired owner of R. and J. Pullman Ltd, leather dressers of London, Godalming and Woodstock, sent him an improved version of his A1 Shield, which was on sale for 25*s.* at the Army and Navy Stores, Harrods and Selfridges.[36] Weighing just under 3 lb, Pullman's shield was made of steel that had been 'government tested and found proof against shrapnel bullets at 700 feet per second velocity, and enemy service revolver at point-blank [range], and against bayonet or lance'. It consisted of four overlapping steel plates that were attached to one another by means of canvas webbing, and provided protection to the chest and abdomen. Each individual plate measured 12 in by 5 in, was curved to fit the contours of the body and was riveted to a stout canvas backing. The shield was secured with adjustable straps at the neck and waist, and when not being worn could be folded up neatly into a canvas or leather case, and carried over the shoulder in the same manner as a haversack.

Roneo Ltd drew Conan Doyle's attention to two designs for bullet-proof body shields that they had produced in association with the Miris Steel Company, which were being tested in the field by 12th Battalion, Gloucestershire Regiment, under the command of Lt Col Martin Archer-Shee, Conservative MP for Finsbury Central (Figure 22).[37] The first was a breastplate shaped to cover the left side of the body – which was more often exposed by an advancing soldier than the front – that provided protection to the heart and abdomen. The second was a large breastplate with shoulder straps and belt that covered the whole of the chest. Both shields were made of $^1/_3$ in steel, which it was claimed would stop a Mauser rifle bullet at 40 yards, and were padded to help absorb the shock of impact.

Some of Conan Doyle's correspondents recognised the problem of the weight of armour plate required to stop a rifle or machine gun bullet, and looked for alternative solutions to the use of steel. Janet Peck, from Mayfair in London, who was appalled by 'the sickening obstinacy with which every obvious necessity is met in the War Office', had an interesting idea.[38] She sent Conan Doyle a sample of vulcanite, a hardened rubber made by the

"I think in this respect we shall revert to the old method of warfare when protection for the body was not regarded as detracting from the valour of a man." MR. LLOYD GEORGE, Secretary of State for War, House of Commons, July 24th, 1916.

The PULLMAN A.1.
SHIELD.

Folded for carrying over the shoulder like a field glass.

This shield is the lightest and most efficient of all steel shields. The steel has been Government tested and found proof against shrapnel bullets at 700 feet per second velocity, any enemy service revolver at point-blank, and against bayonet or lance. All the protection given to the head by the steel helmet supplied in such vast quantities to our Troops is secured to the vital parts of the body, back or front, by this shield. It folds when not in use into a space that enables it to be carried over the shoulder as easily as a pair of field glasses.

Open for use to be worn under the tunic.

Price **25/-** *complete*

(*Patent and registration applied for*)

'Land & Water' says: "It affords the maximum of protection obtainable in any form of shield . . . . one of the best practical shields made."

Selling Agents :—

THE O.W. CUIRASS SYNDICATE,

(33 Fouberts Place)

Entrance : **42 GREAT MARLBOROUGH ST., LONDON, W.**

(Two minutes from Oxford Circus)

21 Advertising leaflet for John Pullman's A1 Shield. Royal Armouries, Conan Doyle Papers.

vulcanisation of natural rubber with sulphur, which she had come across during her investigations into the use of waterproof paper to make smocks for Indian and Canadian troops, who had suffered badly from the conditions on the Western Front before they were issued with great coats. She wondered whether 'a shield could be made of this composition still hardened by greater pressure'.

Conan Doyle even tried to develop his own non-metallic body armour in association with the inventor, industrialist and entrepreneur Herbert Frood. Frood's company, Ferodo, based in Chapel en le Frith in Derbyshire, specialised in the design and manufacture of friction products, and made brake linings for armoured cars, motor vehicles and tanks.

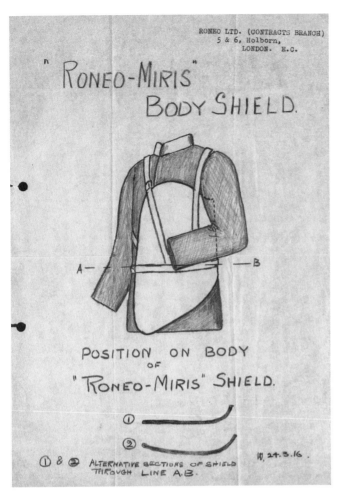

RONEO LTD. (CONTRACTS BRANCH)
5 & 6, Holborn,
LONDON. E.C.

"RONEO-MIRIS"
BODY SHIELD.

A —   — B

POSITION ON BODY
OF
"RONEO-MIRIS" SHIELD.

① ━━━━━

② ━━━━━━

① & ② ALTERNATIVE SECTIONS OF SHIELD
THROUGH LINE A.B.

H. 24.3.16.

22 Sketch of the Roneo–Miris Body Shield. Royal Armouries, Conan Doyle Papers.

A surviving minute book in the Derbyshire Record Office reveals that on 9 August they produced a bullet-proof fabric for Conan Doyle, made of asbestos die-pressed from $^1/_4$ to $^3/_{16}$ in, and boiled in black wax with a 20 per cent carnauba palm wax content.[39]

Conan Doyle acquired one of the Dayfield Body Shields, which had attracted an impressive number of unsolicited testimonials since its introduction in April 1915, and may also have purchased a Chemico Body Shield, which was the leading non-metallic body armour.[40] He was a keen rifleman, and tested all of the armours he received in his garden at Windelsham Manor near Crowborough.[41] His younger sons, Denis and Adrian, were forbidden to come close when their father was engaged in his experiments, but could clearly hear the sounds of bullets being deflected or thudding into their target.[42]

At the end of July 1916 Conan Doyle wrote to the new Secretary of State for War regarding his ideas, and received a response a few days later. Lloyd George assured him that 'I am at the moment paying special attention to the subject of shields', and added 'If you have any ideas on this subject I shall be very grateful if you will let me have them, and you may depend upon it that they shall receive careful consideration.'[43] This was considerably more

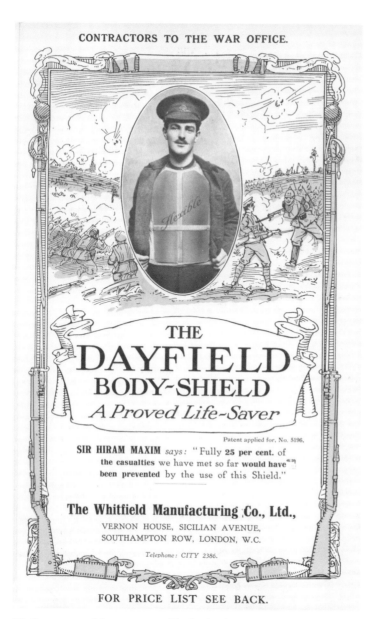

CONTRACTORS TO THE WAR OFFICE.

THE
DAYFIELD
BODY-SHIELD
A Proved Life-Saver

Patent applied for. No. 5196.

SIR HIRAM MAXIM *says:* "Fully **25 per cent.** of **the casualties** we have met so far **would have been prevented** by the use of this Shield."

The Whitfield Manufacturing Co., Ltd.,
VERNON HOUSE, SICILIAN AVENUE,
SOUTHAMPTON ROW, LONDON, W.C.

Telephone: CITY 2386.

FOR PRICE LIST SEE BACK.

23 Front cover of the promotional leaflet for the Dayfield Body Shield. Royal Armouries, Conan Doyle Papers.

information than Sir Edwin Cornwall, Liberal MP for Bethnal Green North East, received on the same day in response to his written question asking if the Secretary of State for War was able to make any comment on the provision of body armour for troops, only to be informed by Henry Forster that he was unable to add anything to his previous statement.[44]

Conan Doyle also wrote to the Chief of the Imperial General Staff, Lt Gen. Sir William Robertson, whom he had met during his service in South Africa, and to whom he had dedicated his history of the *Campaign in France and Flanders*, which was being serialised

24 Sir Arthur Conan Doyle with his two young sons, Denis and Adrian. Conan Doyle Estate.

in the *Strand Magazine*. On 14 August he received a brief letter from Robertson thanking him for sending a copy of his book, promising to look into what could be done concerning body armour, and reminding him that 'I took your previous tip as regards badges for wounded men.'[45] The latter was a reference to another of Conan Doyle's campaigns on behalf of British servicemen, to persuade the War Office to issue wound badges to those who had been injured on active service in recognition of the contribution they had made, and to prevent unfortunate incidents of men who had been discharged from the armed services being presented with white feathers. The campaign would eventually lead to the introduction of the Silver War Badge.

Conan Doyle wrote to Lloyd George again on 8 August, presumably summarising the arguments he had put forward in his letters to *The Times* and the *Observer*, the correspondence he had received, and the tests he had conducted on commercially manufactured body armour, as well as his own attempts to produce a bullet-proof fabric using asbestos. It was several days before the Secretary of State for War replied, and in the meantime Caleb Saleeby kept up the pressure with a series of articles that appeared in the *Daily Post*, the *Daily Chronicle* and the *New Statesman*. He reminded readers that the previous year he and Conan Doyle had suggested that if the authorities were to develop helmets and body armour to protect the vital parts of a soldier's body, then the 'surgeons would go bail for the rest', and that since then (thanks to his successful intervention) a new steel helmet had been produced.[46] He praised the manganese steel developed by Sir Robert Hadfield, and noted that although the helmet weighed 2 lb, it was capable of resisting a bullet fired from a Webley automatic pistol at a range of 5 yards, and was proof against a shrapnel bullet, 41 to the pound, and striking with a velocity of 750 ft per second. He revealed that:

> [w]earing my precious specimen of this helmet, from which I can scarcely bear to be parted at night, and which I owe, as a kind of memento, to the Ministry of Munitions. I have been freely and repeatedly bashed over the head with a heavy poker, without injury. It can be laid on the

25 Dr Caleb Saleeby, science correspondent for the *New Statesman*. Library of Congress.

floor and thus struck with all one's might, and though the line of the blow may be depressed this amazing steel does not give.

Saleeby praised the low profile of the new helmet, with its smooth, rounded and oblique surface ideal for deflecting a projectile; and its double structure, with its outer steel bowl and inner soft cap of felt and wadding, bounded on all sides by rubber studs to protect the head further from concussion, contusion and fracture. Even the surface was roughened and sanded so as not to reflect the rays of the sun or moon. It was just unfortunate, he noted, that British troops suffered from one 'serious, tragic and magnificent fault': they were too brave, and so reluctant to wear their helmets.

Saleeby was critical of the commercially-manufactured helmets and body armour, and called upon shops to withdraw such 'murderous rubbish', which had not been tested and were not made of manganese steel, demanding that the Government prohibit their sale. He was especially critical of one helmet made of corrugated material, which splintered when struck and was 'worse than worthless'. This may well have been the headgear manufactured by Messrs Beckersniff and Co., well-known bakers, which was illustrated in the *Daily Mirror*, and which *Punch* suggested could be used either as a helmet or a wash bowl, or 'employed in the shaping of dainty jellies for the dugout'.[47]

Lens recalled that eight months had passed since he had made the suggestion that the heart should be protected, and the subject of body armour had been raised (presumably a reference to Athelstan Rendall's question in the House of Commons).[48] He praised Conan

PROTECTIVE HELMETS USED BY THE PRINCIPAL BELLIGERENT ARMIES.

THE BRITISH AND AMERICAN HELMETS MADE OF THE " RESISTA " STEEL INVENTED BY HADFIELD OF SHEFFIELD

THE FRENCH HELMET

THE GERMAN HELMET

WEIGHT 25½ OZS.

THE HADFIELD HELMET KEEPS OUT ALL SHRAPNEL BULLETS UP TO A VELOCITY OF 750 F.S. AND OFTEN UP TO 900 F.S. (FEET PER SECOND)

WEIGHT 23¾ OZS.

WEIGHT 37 OZS.

THIS PHOTOGRAPH SHOWS THE STANDARD FRENCH HELMET WHICH IS EASILY PERFORATED BY SHRAPNEL BULLETS AT AS LOW A VELOCITY AS 350 FEET PER SECOND.

THIS GERMAN HELMET ALTHOUGH 12 OZS HEAVIER AND 12% THICKER THAN THE HADFIELD HELMETS IS PERFORATED AT MUCH LOWER VELOCITIES. IN ADDITION IT SUFFERS FROM THE SERIOUS DEFECT OF CRACKING BADLY UNDER IMPACT, AS SHOWN BY THE PHOTOGRAPH.

HADFIELDS LTD
SHEFFIELD.

L/2624

26 Front cover of a promotional leaflet showing the superiority of the British steel helmet produced by Hadfields Ltd, Sheffield. Metropolitan Museum of Art, Bashford Dean Papers.

Doyle's promotion of the issue in *The Times* and the *Observer*, and was convinced that 'when the work is done, as done, I doubt not, it will have to be, it will owe much to his bold and cautious advocacy'. He accepted in principle the argument regarding the weight of body armour, but observed that the heart was particularly vulnerable and exposed in modern warfare, during bayonet fighting, shooting, bomb throwing and so forth, and thus he supported the suggestion made by Conan Doyle for the development of a heart-guard. He called upon the Ministry of Munitions to address the problem of preserving lives that would be needed after the war, and to surpass its previous efforts with the helmet. Lens asked that medical experts be consulted in the design of body armour, and suggested that the Parliamentary Secretary to the Minister of Munitions (Dr Christopher Addison, former Professor of Anatomy at University College, Sheffield) should 'return to his life-work and make a study of the superficial and topographical anatomy of the chest, so as to construct a heart-guard giving the maximum protection to the heart and great blood-vessels with the minimum of inconvenience to respiration and the movements of the pectoral-brachial musculature'.

On 15 August the Minister of Munitions, Edwin Montagu, made a statement to the House of Commons on the work of his department since it had been established in 1915.[49] He drew MPs' attention to the increase in the production of artillery shells and heavy guns, machine guns and rifles, small arms ammunition and explosives. He highlighted the role of the Inspection Department in improving quality control, as well as the work of other departments involved in the design, manufacture and supply of munitions. He also noted the success in improvising new weapons for trench warfare, and observed that 'the Ministry

27 Advertising leaflet for Portobank's 'Best' Body Shield. Metropolitan Museum of Art, Bashford Dean Papers.

has carried out much experimental work with body shields, and we have now some results which are being tested on a large scale in the field'. In the debate that followed, Lt Col Archer-Shee, on leave from the front, reflected on his own experiments with body armour:

> One of the things that seem to be certain is that in open warfare it is almost impossible to use shields that will be of any real use in keeping bullets out, because you cannot so far get a bullet-proof shield that will cover any reasonable part of the body that is under seventeen pounds in weight. Of course, by experiments we might find something lighter, but the lighter forms of shield, which I was told have been adopted by the War Office … have been found by experiment to be almost useless for operations, excepting for trench operations, quite close.

Archer-Shee shared the opinion that the tactical value of body armour was to assist troops in crossing No Man's Land and breaking through the German lines, after which it could be discarded. He was bitter that his own ideas had been rejected, but acknowledged that those who criticised the Ministry of Munitions were unaware of the difficulties involved. As the debate continued into the evening, Lloyd George made his contribution to the subject. He was certain that the practical problems of producing a bullet-proof body armour light enough for a man to carry could be overcome, but that more attention would need to be given to the prejudice of the men against any additional burden. He felt sure, however, that just as the helmet had become accepted, so too would body armour.

Saleeby also received a considerable correspondence following his articles on body armour from soldiers, their friends and relatives, surgeons, inventors, patentees, retailers, and other 'indescribables'.[50] One famous soldier and educator, Lt Gen. Robert Baden-Powell, wrote to thank him for his 'very practical ideas of body armour', and offered the opinion:

> I think that one of the main reasons why soldiers do not readily adopt armour (apart from its appearing to be a sign of funk, apart from the extra pounds to their load where already they feel that the last straw has been reached, apart from the proved danger of inferior shields) is the fact that so much 'rot' has appeared in the newspapers on the subject as makes them feel that the whole question is being ventilated by armchair theorists.

Saleeby felt that soldiers need not be ashamed of protecting themselves, and hoped that any suggestion of cowardice had been overcome by the introduction of the helmet. He considered that the questions of weight and mobility had been dealt with, as Conan Doyle had shown how shields and body armour need be used only for a short time, and had argued that the speed of advance was less important than maintaining sufficient strength to capture and hold an objective. There had been a significant increase in the number of body armours on the market at this time, with advertisements appearing in the press for the Dayfield, Chemico, National, Portobank and Crossman body shields, and Saleeby noted that although some were undoubtedly worth wearing, he agreed with Baden-Powell that others were simply dangerous. He resumed his attack on 'the purveyors of murderous trash', who not only lined their pockets but also prejudiced discussions on the development of effective body armour, although he did note that the director of one Oxford Street store had offered to withdraw any body armours that he chose to condemn. He blamed the capitalist system, which allowed such devices to be produced at a trivial cost and then sold for an exorbitant and often prohibitive amount, and questioned why patentees should benefit when there was almost a total absence of originality in their ideas. He observed that many of his correspondents had asked for his advice on the best body armour to purchase, but he was only able to suggest that they do as he did, and 'walk into the shops, and use their wits'.

Saleeby recalled that he had previously proposed that examples of armour preserved in museums, as well as those evolved by nature, should be studied for inspiration, and noted that one of his correspondents had developed some interesting ideas based on armour he had seen 'in practice in a far-distant land', but gave no further details. He hoped that, following Montagu's statement to the House of Commons, the Ministry of Munitions would now 'most hopefully and gratefully look for the solution of a problem which has no insoluble or even particularly difficult elements, but merely needs, like problems in general, that we shall give our minds to it'.

Lens wrote a more detailed article a few days later to deal with the volume of letters he had received, and to discuss some of the common misconceptions and current abuses.[51] He noted that although the helmet was made of manganese steel, there were many other alloys available, and had previously suggested that the experience of the Royal Navy in the use of different types of steel might be useful in the development of body armour. He wondered if nickel steel, which was used to produce armour plate for warships, might also provide an effective protection against nickel-jacketed rifle and machine gun bullets. He reminded his readers that he was not an expert in this field, and was scathing of those inventors and manufacturers who had written to ask his advice on metallurgical matters, an example of Poulton's 'national neglect of science' made more monstrous by the fact that Britain had led the world in the development of steel since Bessemer's time, and that some of the foremost experts worked in Sheffield.

Lens expressed his concern about the debilitating effect of ignorance, in particular the public's lack of basic knowledge, and the power of information when confined to a few, who could exploit it to their own advantage and the disadvantage of others. He was critical of the patent system, 'the principle of which seems to be to grant patents to everybody and everything', which placed people at the mercy of manufacturers able to advertise their products as 'patent', and to charge as much as they pleased. He was particularly angry at the advertisement for the Dayfield Body Shield, which charged more than twice as much for the double shield as the single, on the spurious grounds that the backplate needed to be made of thicker steel. He was afraid that the same scandalous practice was about to be repeated with body armour as it had with helmets, where 'the prices demanded are monstrous and shameful', and sadly concluded that even in wartime 'Capital must be served or Life may go and be shot.' He noted that two helmets could be purchased for the cost of one War Savings Certificate, and calculated that the cost of making body armour was no more than a few shillings.[52] He felt the situation would only be improved when the Ministry of Munitions produced its own body armour to complement the steel helmet.

Lens was aware of the significant progress that had been made in surgery since the beginning of the war, but nevertheless regarded the success of the steel helmet in reducing the number of head wounds to be 'worth all the surgical marvels in the world'. He had received a large number of letters from military surgeons, all of whom supported the development of body armour or shields, and made a number of valuable suggestions, but he considered it tragic that they had taken so long to consider the prevention of wounds, rather than the cure. He reserved his most bitter condemnation, however, for the education system that had produced Britain's military leaders:

> in practice the most expensive and generally admired in the world, to which our ruling classes are subjected, with its ideals of bodily cleanliness, physical courage, mental crassness and moral cowardice. The ideal of bodily elegance and insouciance, admirable in itself, leads to the reckless and foolish and useless sacrifice of hosts of splendid and much needed young lives.

Lens considered that such attitudes had already cost thousands of lives, and he condemned one famous British general, Lord Kitchener, who had stated that in his opinion 'medical advice is a very good thing – when it is asked for'. He was convinced that Britain would win the war, but was concerned that if the loss of lives continued, she would lack the manpower resources to benefit from the peace.

Conan Doyle, Saleeby and their fellow campaigners were naturally unaware that considerable efforts had been made to provide British troops with better protection. Shortly after receiving Conan Doyle's second letter, Lloyd George was sent a copy of a report written by Arthur McDougall Duckham, the Deputy Comptroller of Munitions Supply and a member of the sub-committee on body armour.[53] Duckham reviewed the various types of body armour then in existence, and summarised the results of tests and trials conducted to date. He divided armour into two classes, those that were shrapnel-proof and those that

28 Field Marshal Horatio Herbert Kitchener, 1st Earl Kitchener, Lord Kitchener, Secretary of State for War (1914–16). Library of Congress.

were bullet-proof, and then sub-divided each class according to whether they were metal, non-metallic or a compound of the two.

Duckham observed that experiments on metal armour to give protection against shrapnel, bomb fragments, spent bullets or bayonet thrusts had shown that manganese steel with a covering of fabric gave the best results. Tests on non-metallic materials, such as vulcanised fibre, compressed paper asbestos, rubber, woven fabrics, cotton wool and other fibres (either alone or treated with resins or gum, celluloid or mica) had shown that with the exception of silk none gave better results weight-for-weight than steel. Duckham reported that it was generally believed that the use of non-metallic shields would be adversely affected by vermin and moisture, although he did note that silk had been used in the Bomber's Necklet and was also being tested by the Royal Flying Corps. He observed that tests on compound armour made of metal plates, mail, or woven wires embedded in, faced with or backed with non-metallic materials had also proved unsatisfactory, and there were fears that, when perforated, fragments of the protective material carried into the body might cause more serious or even fatal wounds. Similar concerns were expressed to a lesser extent about metallic armour, and Duckham concluded that overall the tests carried out to date had shown that manganese steel gave the best protection against shrapnel, but nickel or chrome–nickel steel gave the best results against rifle and machine gun fire at close range. He noted that a body armour made of manganese steel and covered in khaki drill was currently being evaluated in France, and that a 'bullet-proof breastplate' had also been sent to GHQ for consideration.

Duckham then summarised the experiments that had been carried out to produce a shield that was bullet-proof, and noted that it had very quickly become clear that steel was the only suitable material for such a device. Tests had shown that a steel plate no less than 10 mm thick and weighing about 16 lb per square foot would give full protection against concentrated machine gun fire at close ranges, and a steel plate 7 mm thick and weighing 11 lb per square foot would give protection against rifle fire and scattered machine gun fire. The weight of such shields made them difficult to move over rough terrain, however, and he noted that no mobile shield had been successfully tested 'which could be used with any degree of efficiency over trenches or ground broken up with shell craters'. Duckham concluded that the options seemed to be to develop either a portable shield made of 7 mm steel plate or a power-driven mobile shield. He did note, however, that 'It would of course be possible to use 7 mm plate attached to the tunic of the soldier covering vital spots'.

Lloyd George was also advised of the results of the field trials that had recently been carried out in France of the heavy model of the Dayfield Body Shield and the MID Bomber's Shield. GHQ had rejected the Dayfield as too heavy and cumbersome, and asked for 400

29 MID Bomber's Shield and Necklet, adopted in 1916. Metropolitan Museum of Art, Bashford Dean Papers.

modified sets of the Bomber's Shield to be issued to every division in France and Flanders.[54] A few days later a memo confirmed that an order had been placed for 50,000 shields.[55]

When Lloyd George finally responded to Conan Doyle on 2 September he was able to inform him that serious efforts were being made to develop body armour, although he observed that:

> strange to say, our great difficulty is to get the soldiers at the Front to take them into use. Even with the steel helmet there was a considerable amount of grumbling when they were called upon to wear it, and it is only experience which has taught them the very great value and safety given by it, and now as you know, they will not do so [go into battle] without the steel helmet.[56]

He had to admit that the production of bullet-proof body armour remained difficult 'without throwing an impossible weight on the soldier', but noted that a shrapnel-proof armour had been 'tried at the Front with such success that a large number of them have been asked for and are in the course of supply'. He assured Conan Doyle that he would not lose sight of the matter, and promised to discuss it with Haig when he visited France in the next few days (the meeting subsequently took place on 12 September).

On 3 September Conan Doyle's nephew, Capt. Alec Forbes, 2nd Battalion, Royal Warwickshire Regiment, was killed in action at Ginchy. Conan Doyle continued to lobby for the development of bullet-proof body armour, and took the opportunity of a further letter to *The Times* on the subject of a captured German report, which had acknowledged the qualities of British soldiers and the superiority of some of their equipment, to add as a final observation that 'it is for us to add to our advantages those protective devices, whether shields or armour, which seem to me to be the most vital problem of all'.[57] He also

30 Sir Douglas Haig, Marshal Joffre and Lloyd George meeting in France during the Battle of the Somme, 12 September 1916. Mary Evans Picture Library.

Wounded Soldier (seeing a body-shield in shop window). "No, I
DON'T THINK MUCH O' THEM THINGS. A MATE O' MINE 'AD ONE AND
A BIT O' SHRAPNEL GLANCED OFF IT AND CAUGHT ME IN THE ARM."

31 Cartoon by George Morrow, *Punch*, 21 October 1916. Punch Ltd.

wrote to a number of influential figures including Winston Churchill.[58] The advocates of
body armour must have been delighted when a few days later Henry Forster responded to
a question asked by Richard Hazleton, MP for North Galway, on the present state of investigations and experiments into body armour with the news that 'a report on the subject
has been received from Sir Douglas Haig, and steps are being taken to meet his wishes'.[59]
Although Forster declined to give any further details it must have appeared to Conan
Doyle that the long campaign to provide protection for British troops had been successful
at least in part.

The design of the new shrapnel-proof or light body shield had been successfully developed by the MID and the Munitions Design Council in little more than six months, and
an order for 10,000 units had been placed in February even before field trials were complete. Unfortunately production of the Bomber's Shield was slow, and in a memo dated
8 November, John MacIntosh, Director of the Trench Weapons Supply Department, was
forced to admit that only 7,000 had been shipped from the initial order.[60] He reported that
the delivery of the balance had commenced the previous week, and promised that weekly
deliveries would follow.

There were still those who remained to be convinced, and *Punch* echoed the concerns of many when it published a cartoon of a wounded soldier, who on seeing a body shield on sale in a shop window remarked to his fair companion: 'No, I don't think much o' them things. A mate o' mine 'ad one and a bit o' shrapnel glanced off it and caught me in the arm.'[61] A triumphant Saleeby was in no doubt, however, that 'the principle of armour, which no one questioned until modern times, and against which nothing but the cheapest nonsense about funk can now be said' had finally been accepted, and the military's prejudice against such devices overcome.[62] He trusted that the ethical dilemma facing officers, who could secretly fortify themselves against the dangers which their men were exposed to, would soon no longer arise.

Saleeby continued to be critical of commercially manufactured body armour made from poor-quality steel, and hoped that the experiments of the Ministry of Munitions would finally put an end to the 'amateurism and competition amongst private firms'. He repeated his condemnation of the outrageous prices they charged, and hoped that the announcement made in the House of Commons would terminate the period of 'exploitation and incompetence'. His disapproval, however, did not prevent Alfred Byrne, the Irish Parliamentary Party MP for Dublin Harbour, from asking the Secretary of State of War a few days later 'whether the Government have considered the advisability of serving troops with the body shields that are now on exhibition in London; if he will say whether the shields have been tested by the War Office; and, if so, with what result?'.[63] Henry Forster confirmed that the Ministry of Munitions was considering the question of testing some of the commercially produced body armour, but refrained from providing any details on tests that had already been carried out.

Saleeby was granted permission by the Ministry of Munitions to exhibit the Mark I Steel Helmet, the Bomber's Necklet, and the Bomber's Shield to selected audiences in London and Sheffield, although he was under strict instructions not to publish any of its secrets.[64] Lens believed that the new body armour would 'effectively conserve our military and industrial man-power in a degree affording high service to speedy and complete victory', and hoped 'We shall all be seeing them soon at the pictures.'[65] He praised the work of the MID, but continued to press for research into protecting the heart and major blood vessels against rifle and machine gun fire, and continued his attack on commercial manufacturers of body armour who '... put murderous ... rubbish on the market, at thieves' prices, and thus teach the practical soldier, who is dying for them in the trenches, to regard armour as a death-trap, so that the provision and use of practical armour is fatally prevented or delayed'.

He did acknowledge that some of the body armours had merit, and made special note of the resisting power of one that was made in Birmingham of non-metallic materials (the Chemico Body Shield), but although it held many advantages he felt that the wet conditions prevailing in the trenches would probably render it ineffective. In July, at the Royal Institute of Public Health in London, Saleeby exhibited the new body armour; the steel helmet; the silk necklet; and the mail visor that had been issued to infantry and tank crews to protect their eyes from pieces of rock, sand or metal splinters.[66]

Conan Doyle had two further opportunities to press his case for bullet-proof body armour. On 7 February 1917 he had lunch with Lloyd George, his secretary (Frances Stevenson) and Col Stern, at which the new Prime Minister asked him to write his official biography.[67] Conan Doyle politely declined, saying that he was too busy writing his history, and that he had never written a biography. Unfortunately there is no detailed record of what else they discussed, but it would be surprising if the subject of body armour was not raised. Then, in April, Conan Doyle was invited to breakfast at 10 Downing

Street. He later remembered that it was an informal affair, and while the Prime Minister poured out the tea, he helped himself to bacon and eggs, and then served the same to Lloyd George. They discussed a wide range of subjects, including the great loss the country had sustained by the death of Lord Kitchener, the role played by the 38th Welsh Division in the capture of Mametz Wood during the Battle of the Somme, the progress of Conan Doyle's history and his opinions on various generals he had met in France, as well as the revolution in Russia. Conan Doyle recalled that he spoke to the Prime Minister 'about my views as to the use of armour, and found him very keen upon it. He is an excellent listener, and seems honestly interested in what you say. He said he had no doubt that in the problem of armour lay the future of warfare, but how to carry it was the crux. He said that the soldiers always obstructed the idea – which was my experience also.'[68]

Lloyd George mentioned that he was about to have another meeting at which the subject of body armour would be discussed, and as Conan Doyle was leaving Downing Street, he suddenly sat down in one of the hall chairs, much to the surprise of the butler who was accompanying him, and wrote out a few notes, which he asked to be delivered to the Prime Minister. This was his final act in the campaign. He seems to have been reassured that the matter was finally in hand, and besides, he was fully engaged at this time in writing his history, and a new series of Sherlock Holmes adventures to boost the morale of the British public.[69]

The subject of body armour was discussed at the meeting of the War Cabinet on 22 March, and the Minister of Munitions, Dr Addison, and the Master General of the Ordnance, Maj. Gen. W. T. Furse, showed several different types, most of which were not proof against machine gun fire at close range.[70] The following month the Secretary of State for War submitted a memo in which he noted that the Field Marshal Commanding in Chief in France had reported that although the Bomber's Shield had shown some value in trench warfare, it was considered too heavy for use in an advance.[71] Further reports had therefore been called for regarding the value of a lighter pattern of body armour, and the efficacy of armour in general. In June both Haig and Lt Gen. Frederick Stanley Maude in Mesopotamia confirmed that the Bomber's Shield had been used with some success by bombers, patrols and sentries, but was too heavy and awkward for use in large-scale attacks.[72] In addition, Haig reported that the army commanders had expressed a preference for the 'later and lighter design of body armour', and requested that 200 of these be issued to every division.

The precise history of the development of the Experimental Ordnance Board (EOB) Body Armour is unknown, but a detailed evaluation of the Dayfield and Chemico Body Shields had been conducted by the MID in February, and it seems natural to assume that the design was based on the findings of the report.[73] The EOB Body Armour consisted of front, back and abdomen plates; was made of 18-gauge manganese steel, heavily padded and covered in tan-coloured canvas; and weighed 6 lb 8 oz. It was secured with leather straps and buckles, and offered the wearer protection against pistol bullets, shrapnel and grenade fragments. Production of the new body armour was slow, however, and when in January 1918 Arthur Lynch, Irish Parliamentary Party MP for Clare West, asked the Under-Secretary of State for War, James MacPherson, if all soldiers had now received the new equipment, he was informed rather disingenuously that 'the whole of the troops at the front are not provided with body shields, but all demands of the Commander-in-Chief have been met'.[74] MPs continued to ask questions on the subject, and a few months later MacPherson fended off a further enquiry from Leslie Scott, Conservative MP for Liverpool Exchange. Scott asked if the Government would consider issuing the Chemico Body Shield, which had successfully resisted both bullets and shrapnel, to all officers and men, only to be informed

32 EOB Body Armour, adopted in 1917, and Bomber's Necklet. Metropolitan Museum of Art, Bashford Dean Papers.

that 'other forms of body armour have been found more satisfactory, and have consequently been issued in preference to the Chemico body-shield'.[75]

In August 1918 the Allies launched a series of offensives on the Western Front that forced the Germans to abandon the Hindenburg Line, and brought the period of trench warfare to an end. Nevertheless, in the same month, Winston Churchill, who had returned to the Government as Minister of Munitions the previous year, formed a sub-committee consisting of members of the Trench Warfare Department and the Munitions Inventions Department to look into the future requirements of equipment to be used in trench warfare, including body armour. Saleeby, with the help of Sir Alfred Keogh, Director General of the Army Medical Services, placed all the information he had collated, as well as the models and examples he had acquired, before the Committee at the Royal Society of Medicine.[76] The Committee considered which material should be used to provide body armour, and reflected that to date no steel had been produced with sufficient resisting power and lightness that was proof against rifle and machine gun fire.[77] It judged that to give complete protection against standard ammunition (not armour-piercing bullets) would require armour plate of a weight of 10 lb per square foot, and that such heavy armour precluded its general use. It concluded, however, that light armour would greatly reduce the casualties caused by shrapnel wounds to the most vulnerable areas, and that silk would provide effective protection to other parts of the body. It then investigated which parts of the body were most in need of protection, and determined that the most vulnerable area was the chest, where the heart and the roots of the major blood vessels were located, and where a penetrative wound was almost always fatal. The Committee looked into an idea to place a steel plate at the back of the box respirator (gas mask) to protect the region of the heart, which had been submitted by Capt. Kenneth Walker, Royal Army Medical Corps, and investigated the possibility of using an entrenching tool, which the infantry carried in large-scale attacks to help them dig in, the shovel blade of which would form a breastplate. By this time, however, the armistice had been declared, and the Trench Warfare Department was in the process of closing down.[78]

CONCLUSION

Arthur Conan Doyle's suggestions on body armour and shields, and Caleb Saleeby's ideas on helmets and body armour, were a thoughtful response to the heavy casualties being suffered by British troops, given the unusual circumstances brought about by trench warfare. Even before the first campaign had begun in July 1915 the value of the steel helmet in reducing the number of head wounds had been recognised, and work had been undertaken to develop an effective British design. Saleeby showed a clear understanding of the requirements and the need for careful experimentation, and is generally credited with playing a major role in its introduction. The need for additional protection in the form of body armour and shields was hotly disputed, however, by those who argued that such devices would be too heavy for a man to carry, and that the additional weight, when added to the burden already carried by soldiers, would result in a loss of mobility. Doubts were also raised as to whether such protection would be effective against rifle and machine gun fire, and concerns were expressed that the fragmentation of the plates or deformation of the bullet might present an additional risk of more serious or even fatal wounds. Some of those in favour agreed that the development of effective bullet-proof body armour was unlikely, and perhaps even dangerous to the wearer, but felt that shrapnel-proof body armour could be produced. Others were convinced that science and ingenuity could overcome the practical problems. Conan Doyle was aware that the weight of steel plate might be prohibitive, and argued that if complete body armour could not be provided then the protection of the head, heart and other vital organs would save lives. He also suggested that mobile shields could be developed to provide complete protection to troops attacking heavily defended positions. By the end of 1915 it must have appeared that his pleas had fallen on deaf ears, as nothing seemed to have been done, but in actual fact serious efforts were being made to develop all manner of devices to provide protection to the troops.

The delivery of the first million helmets to the British Army in France and Flanders was completed by the first week of July 1916, but as the Battle of the Somme continued to rage and losses mounted, the debate was renewed. The second campaign was marked by increasing resentment on the one side at the interference of armchair generals, and by frustration on the other at the apparent lack of progress made by the War Office and the Ministry of Munitions in addressing the problem, and the failure of the Army to adapt to the situation on the Western Front. Conan Doyle continued to maintain that the unique nature of trench warfare made the objections to the use of body armour and shields irrelevant, and even put forward his own ideas to the tactical problem of ensuring that the attacking infantry reached the enemy lines in sufficient strength to capture and secure their objectives. He received welcome support from Saleeby, who agreed that body armour was urgently required, and pointed to the undoubted success of steel helmets, once the reluctance of the troops to wear them had been overcome. The number of commercially-produced body armours had proliferated since the beginning of the year, and Saleeby became increasingly critical of their quality and expense, as well as their prejudicial effect on the confidence of the troops in such devices and on the debate in general, and called upon the Government to ban their sale. Conan Doyle was equally suspicious about the usefulness of the body armour available for private purchase, and recognised the ethical dilemma of officers who could afford to buy such protection when it was denied to their men.

Unknown to all but a privileged few, the military authorities had agreed to the development of a light body armour at the end of 1915, although many senior officers, including Haig, remained highly sceptical of the value of such equipment, and refused to consider their employment in large numbers. A practical design for a Bomber's Shield was successfully produced by the MID and the Munitions Design Department, and 50,000 were ordered in August 1916. The development of portable shields was less successful, and although two designs for mobile shields were approved should such equipment ever be requested, these devices had already been superseded by the development of the tank, which made its first appearance at the Battle of Flers–Courcelette in September 1916. Unfortunately the production of the body armour was a low priority in comparison with the production of aircraft and tanks, artillery shells and heavy guns, machine guns and rifles, small arms ammunition and explosives. Little more than half of the order for the MID Bomber's Shield was delivered, and only 20,000 of the EOB Body Armours, which were adopted to replace it in June 1917, had been sent to France and Flanders by August 1918, when the deadlock on the Western Front was finally broken.[1]

Conan Doyle and Saleeby's precise influence on events is difficult to determine. Nevertheless, there is enough evidence to suggest that between them they created considerable interest in the press, inspired inventors to develop solutions to save lives, influenced MPs to raise the issue in Parliament, and caused ministers to ask questions of officials at the Ministry of Munitions and the War Office. Lloyd George took an interest in Conan Doyle's ideas, and was prepared to engage him in conversation; Saleeby was allowed not only to examine the results of various tests that had been carried out, but also to exhibit examples of the steel helmet, body armour and other protective devices developed to selected audiences. Conan Doyle appears to have been satisfied, following his breakfast meeting with Lloyd George, that the development of bullet-proof body armour was in hand, and may have taken solace in the abandonment of the costly mass infantry attacks, and the successful development of new tactics and equipment such as the tank. In November 1917 he wrote a brief letter to Col Stern acknowledging the success of tanks in the Battle of Cambrai, and the following year, during another visit to the Western Front, he witnessed an attack by the Australian and Canadian divisions 'with the tanks leading the British line, as Boadicea's chariots did of old'.[2] Saleeby, however, was very disappointed at the 'tentative provision' of body armour that had been made, and ultimately regretted that he had 'spent so much thought and labour and time so fruitlessly'.[3]

POSTSCRIPT

The most detailed analysis of helmets and body armour during the First World War was conducted by Bashford Dean, Curator of Armor at the Metropolitan Museum of Art, New York, who had urged in 1915 that Conan Doyle's ideas for body armour and shields should 'be seriously considered by the British authorities'.[1] When the United States entered the war in 1917, he was commissioned as a major in the US Army Ordnance Department, and sent to Europe to secure information, samples, specifications and blueprints on all manner of trench weapons and equipment.[2] Dean met with Mr William A. Taylor and Capt. C. H. Ley – who had carried out many of the tests on steel plates and other materials on behalf of the MID and Munitions Design Department in London – and Intendant-General

33 Maj. Bashford Dean, US Army Ordnance Department and Curator of Armor. Metropolitan Museum of Art, Bashford Dean Papers.

August-Louis Adrian in Paris, as well as officers on the general staffs of the American, British and French armies before returning to New York to write his report. Dean was subsequently asked to work on the development of protective equipment for the US Army, and produced a series of prototype helmets with the help of Daniel Tachaux, armourer at the Metropolitan Museum of Art, and other members of staff.[3] Unfortunately the military authorities in the United States proved as conservative as their British counterparts. In 1920, Dean published a study titled *Helmets and body armor in modern warfare*, based on his wartime research, which remains the best work on the subject, and his archive contains a wealth of valuable material for those wishing to research this.[4]

Appendix I

THE OFFICIAL DEVELOPMENT OF BODY ARMOUR AND SHIELDS

The following summary is based largely on the minutes of the Trench Warfare Section (TWS) of the Munitions Design Committee, which from December 1915 to January 1917 was responsible for making recommendations on trench warfare supplies to the Director General of Munitions Design for his final decision.[1]

THE MID BOMBER'S SHIELD

As a result of Haig's request the TWS of the Munitions Design Committee quickly looked into the development of light body armour that would afford all-round protection; would not interfere with the free use of both arms, or impede the movements of the wearer; and would not be too heavy so as to tire men engaged in duties of a prolonged and arduous nature (such as throwing grenades).[2] They began by examining detailed information, supplied by the medical authorities in France, on the incidence and location of wounds. The figures showed that the most common causes of injuries were shell and trench mortar fire (63.5 per cent of serious wounds and 67.9 per cent of slight wounds), followed by rifle and machine gun fire (30.5 per cent and 24.9 per cent), and then by bombs and grenades (6 per cent and 7.2 per cent).[3] They further revealed that the three most vulnerable areas of the body were the head, face and neck; the legs; and the shoulders and back. Injuries to the chest and abdomen were common serious wounds, but the least likely slight wounds, although these figures may be a little misleading given the high instance of wounds to multiple areas.

The TWS then reviewed the results of tests carried out at Wembley Park, London, on various materials and coverings to discover which ones offered the best protection. These indicated that silk showed great potential for protection against shrapnel, and indeed a protective collar, known as the Bomber's Necklet, made of layers of compressed silk, covered in khaki drill and worn over the shoulders to protect the neck and sides of the head, would be issued in July 1915, 400 to each division in France. The report felt, however, that the use of silk was rendered prohibitive by the price and by its liability to deterioration through dirt and wet, as well as by the conflicting demands of cartridge manufacture. It therefore recommended that 18-gauge steel plate from Firth, Whitworth or Hadfields, or other high-quality steel, should be used to make up light body shields, and that they should be made in plaques jointed on the same principle as the Dayfield Body Shield, and covered in khaki drill. The TWS ordered samples of two designs of a Bomber's Shield consisting of front and back plates, with front and back aprons, based on the design of the heavy model of the Dayfield Body Shield, one with a 42 in chest (Type A), and the other with a 38 in chest (Type B), for further testing, with the view that if these proved successful they would be adopted as patterns for subsequent manufacture.

A	Front and back plates, front and back aprons	40 in, 15 lb 8 oz
B	Front and back plates, front and back aprons	38 in, 13 lb 4 oz
C	Front and back plates only	17 in, 6 lb
D	Front plate only	17 in, 3 lb 1 oz

The results of the tests of the Bomber's Shield against grenade fragments at Wembley Park on 11 February 1916 indicated that the best protection was provided by Hadfields Water-Cooled (HWC) 'Era' manganese steel, and that on average 94.5 per cent of the hits from fragments of grenades exploded within 12 feet failed to perforate the plates.[4] Further samples were then produced for extended grenade-throwing tests at Clapham Common on 23 February, together with two additional designs, one consisting of front and back plates (Type C), and the other of just a front plate (Type D), which may have been based on the original model of the Dayfield Body Shield (see table). The report noted that all four types were comfortable to wear, but concluded that the extra protection offered by Types A and B outweighed the slight drawback caused by their extra weight. Several changes were suggested to the design, which reduced the overall weight by about 2 lb, and an order for 5,000 of each type was placed on 25 February for field trials in France.[5] On 26 April the HWC plates were tested against shrapnel bullets, 41 to the pound, and were proved against projectiles with a velocity of 1,100 ft per second.

The Bomber's Shield was made of HWC 18-gauge manganese steel, and weighed about 14 lb. It consisted of front and back plates, arranged in plaques similar to the Dayfield Body Shield, to which were attached additional plates to protect the abdomen and buttocks. Several changes were requested as a result of the trials: lowering the waist strap and adding another higher up to prevent the corners of the shield from opening out, and shortening the braces, which even when fully adjusted were still too long. GHQ also asked that the top corners of the backplate be hollowed out so that they did not catch the bomber's arm in the act of throwing, although this may not have been carried out, as the stamps for the shields had already been made.

PORTABLE SHIELDS

A design for a portable shield fitted with a loophole on the right side, which could either be hung from the shoulders to provide protection for the body, or propped upright on the ground, had been produced by the War Office in May 1915, but in field trials had failed to stop either the German 'S' bullet (penetrated at the fourth shot) or the reversed bullet (penetrated at the first shot).[6] In early December 1915, the War Office wrote to GHQ and reported that a modified version had subsequently been produced, covered with $1/_8$ in Woodite, which was proof against the German reversed bullet, but was considered impracticable, as it weighed over 20 lb.[7]

After Haig's intervention a new design was produced in January 1916, which was made of $1/_4$ in steel and was available in two sizes, the first measuring 18 in long by $13^1/_2$ in wide and weighing $18^3/_4$ lb, and the second measuring 18 in long by 13 in wide and weighing $17^5/_8$ lb.[8] It had a metal prop attached to the back, which served as a handgrip, and enabled the shield to be propped upright at an angle of 60 degrees, and a loophole and shutter in the upper right-hand quarter. The latter was later removed, with a subsequent reduction in the weight of approximately 2 lb, and the front face covered with Woodite instead, which proved successful not only in preventing splinters, but also in giving protection against the German reversed bullet at 50 yards.[9] Samples of the design were sent to France, but GHQ was of the opinion that although undoubtedly useful in certain circumstances, the weight of the shields prohibited their use in actual fighting.[10]

In April 1916 the TWS reviewed another design for a loopholed portable shield made of 10 mm mild steel, weighing 30 lb, and fitted with a light backstay and legs, as well as projections so that the plates could be connected together.[11] It was assumed that a man could carry one or even two plates in an emergency, and that a number of men so equipped would quickly be able to construct a breastwork or use the plates to block a trench. The TWS recommended that some form of attachment be added to the top of the backstay of the shields to enable them to be slung from the shoulder. Tests showed that the shields were proof against the German 'S' bullet at short range, but not the reversed bullet, although the report concluded that increasing the thickness of the plate to 11 mm would provide protection against the latter.[12] Samples made of 11 mm mild steel were sent to France in August 1916 and were compared with a portable shield designed by Chiba Chosaki, President of the Nihon Budo Kai (Japanese Samurai Society) that had been used with some success during the Russo-Japanese War.[13] Both shields were rejected, but despite the fact that the Japanese design failed to stop the German 'S' bullet at ranges of less than 35 yards, and was completely ruined by between seven and ten shots at longer ranges, GHQ asked that a further 200 examples be supplied for further trials, but made of the best British steel.[14] The modified Japanese shields were 19 in long by 12 in wide, and had a niche about 4 in deep and 1 in wide in the right-hand side, instead of the original central loophole. The results of the field trials on the modified shield do not appear to have survived, but they were evidently not adopted for use.[15]

MOBILE SHIELDS

It had become evident as a result of the early development of mobile shields by the Royal Naval Air Service at Wormwood Scrubs, and the work of the Iron Structures Section at the Department of Fortifications and Works, that the weight of such shields prevented their

34 Design for a mobile shield adopted as an official pattern in 1917. Metropolitan Museum of Art, Bashford Dean Papers.

rapid movement over rough terrain, and that the wheels or rollers quickly became mired in soft ground. Nevertheless in April 1916 the sub-committee on body armour, which consisted of members of the Munitions Inventions Department, the Munitions Design Department, the Trench Warfare Supply Department and the Royal Army Medical Corps, inspected two designs for mobile shields. The first was capable of covering five men, and consisted of a steel plate 5 ft 6 in long by 3 ft 7 in high and 10 mm thick, mounted on two large wheels, which also provided some protection from flanking fire.[16] It weighed about 600 lb. The sub-committee saw it tested on good ground by a crew of three men, and were impressed with how easily it moved. They made several suggestions for improvements: fitting a flange that projected outward from the wheels, moving the ball bearings to take the axle to the outside of the wheels, fastening handles to the inside of the wheels to assist the crew in turning them, and fixing a leg or trail to prevent the shield being turned on its axis by concentrated fire once it had been dropped in position. It was subsequently accepted as an official pattern in case a demand for such a shield should be received from the armies in the field.

The second design was capable of protecting 15 men, and consisted of a front shield measuring 6 ft wide by 5 ft high, fitted with a platform capable of mounting a machine gun, and two wings each measuring 10 ft 4 in long by 4 ft 6 in high (rising to 5 ft high at the junction with the front shield), which could either be pushed out or drawn in to provide protection from flanking fire.[17] It used the pedrail wheel invented by Bramah Joseph Diplock, and was propelled by winding two handles. It weighed about 3,000 lb. The sub-committee saw it tested on good ground with crews of 6 and 12 men and, as in the case of the smaller mobile shield, recommended to the TWS that the design be accepted as a pattern in case the armies in the field made a request for such a shield. The TWS concurred, and further recommended that the pedrail shields and other designs be brought forward in due course for inspection by representatives from the Army in France and Flanders, but the development of the tank had made such devices obsolete.

35 Design for a mobile shield mounted with a Vickers machine gun adopted as an official pattern in 1917. Metropolitan Museum of Art, Bashford Dean Papers.

SOLDIER'S BODY SHIELD
(DAYFIELD PATENT DESIGN).
WITH PLATES MADE OF HADFIELD'S "RESISTA" BULLET-PROOF STEEL.
ADOPTED BY THE BRITISH ARMY

SOLDIER'S BODY SHIELD
(DAYFIELD PATENT DESIGN).
WITH PLATES MADE OF HADFIELD'S "RESISTA" BULLET-PROOF STEEL.
ADOPTED BY THE BRITISH ARMY

HADFIELDS LTD SHEFFIELD.

HADFIELDS LTD SHEFFIELD.

36 Promotional images of the original and heavy model of the Dayfield Body Shield produced by Hadfields Ltd, Sheffield. Picture Sheffield.

Appendix II

THE DAYFIELD AND CHEMICO BODY SHIELDS

The original model of the Dayfield Body Shield was designed by Frances Dayton and Ernest Albert Whitfield, and made by the Whitfield Manufacturing Company of London. It consisted of a breastplate and a backplate, each composed of four rectangular manganese steel plaques, covered in khaki drill with metal bands taped over the unprotected seams, but was subsequently modified by extending the front plates up to the shoulders and shaping them at the neck to provide more effective protection.[1] It was claimed to be proof against bayonet, sword, lance, spent bullets, shrapnel, shell splinters and grenade fragments, and was even endorsed by Hiram Maxim, who believed that 'fully twenty-five percent of the casualties we have met so far could have been prevented by the use of this shield'.[2] It was widely advertised for sale as either a single shield weighing 3 lb to protect the chest (21s.), or a double shield weighing 5 lb 8 oz to protect the chest and back (52s. 6d.).

A heavy model of the Dayfield Body Shield was produced specifically for field trials in France in 1916.[3] It was designed with larger breastplates and backplates, composed of six plaques, that extended the protected area to the sides of the body; a large front apron composed of two plaques to cover the abdomen; a single large back apron to cover the rump; and a separate groin-guard.[4] It weighed between 14 and 18 lb, however, and when the field trials were completed it was rejected as too heavy and cumbersome.[5] Nevertheless, the original model continued to be popular as a private purchase for officers, and when a group of overseas MPs visited Hadfields Ltd in Sheffield, Sir George Foster, the Canadian Minister of Trade and Commerce, was photographed wearing a steel helmet and heavy model Dayfield Body Shield.[6]

The first reference to the Chemico Body Shield appeared in May 1916, when a news item in the Birmingham newspapers noted that a new type of body armour had been successfully tested against a .455 Colt revolver and a bayonet, and this was followed a few days later by a report of a similar demonstration at Anderson's Hotel in London.[7] It was invented by Wilfrid Hill of the County Chemical Company in Birmingham, and Joseph Wilks, a draper from Uttoxeter, and took the form of a padded waistcoat stuffed with layers of tissue and scraps of linen, cotton and silk, which were hardened by a resinous material and covered with khaki-coloured muslin.[8] It weighed 4 lb 13 oz. The front shield alone cost 27s. 6d.; the front, side and back shield 47s. 6d.; and there was additional protection for the abdomen available for an extra 10s. 6d. The company claimed that the Chemico was absolutely proof against revolver bullets; spent rifle bullets; sword, bayonet or lance thrust; flying shrapnel; and bursting grenade fragments, and pointed out that there were no metal plates to deflect projectiles into unprotected parts of the body, or to splinter or fracture and so cause more serious wounds. In addition they maintained that the shield was antiseptic and vermin-proof, and could be worn as a garment, and so was not dead weight to be carried. It therefore gave the maximum protection for the minimum weight.

37 Dayfield Body Shield (light model) with the khaki drill removed showing the effects of tests against shrapnel bullets. Metropolitan Museum of Art, Bashford Dean Papers.

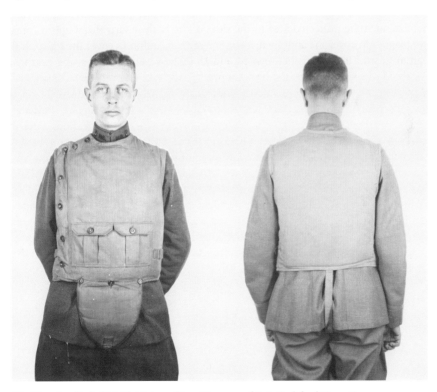

38 Chemico Body Shield. Metropolitan Museum of Art, Bashford Dean Papers.

The Dayfield and Chemico Body Shields attracted considerable interest from the press, and both Whitfield and County Chemicals were quick to use the letters they received from soldiers whose lives had been saved in their advertisements and promotional literature. As a result of their success, when research was being undertaken at the beginning of 1917 into the replacement of the MID Bomber's Shield examples of both armours were purchased from the Army and Navy Stores (for £2 12s. 6d. and £3 3s. respectively) to undergo further official tests.[9] The report concluded that neither shield gave protection against close-range rifle and machine gun fire, whether from normal or glancing shots, and that although both gave considerable protection against shrapnel, bomb fragments, revolver bullets and bayonet thrusts, weight-for-weight the Dayfield offered better defence than the Chemico. The main objection to the Dayfield was that a rifle or machine gun bullet was somewhat deformed when the plates were perforated, and so the resulting wound would probably be much worse than if there had been no protection at all, whereas the Chemico did not appreciably deform a bullet. The report considered that the Chemico was more flexible than the Dayfield, and would also serve as additional clothing, but there were greater hygienic concerns if it got saturated with water, which probably made it unsuitable for use in the trenches.

The report considered that if light body armour was deemed desirable in the present conditions of trench warfare (and steel was not condemned on account of its tendency to deform rifle bullets) then the manganese steel Dayfield was probably the best shield for the purpose. It went on to note that if the requirement of stopping high-velocity bullets were dropped, and the steel made thinner than 18-gauge, then the risk of the bullet deforming would be lessened without seriously decreasing the amount of protection offered against shrapnel and bomb fragments, and the weight would be reduced. The report expressed concern that the metal bands taped over the unprotected seams of the Dayfield were a major weakness, and suggested that a better form of joint should be devised. In actual fact, an improved version of the Dayfield, consisting of a breastplate formed of four overlapping plates riveted together, with a single curved plate or apron covering the abdomen, and weighing 6 lb 8 oz, had been patented, but does not appear to have been tested.[10]

If non-metallic body armour was considered preferable then the report judged that better results would be obtained by using silk rather than the Chemico form of protection. It noted that silk provided better protection against shrapnel and other low-velocity blunt projectiles than steel, but that fabric was less effective against sharper projectiles. Furthermore, silk would not compare favourably with steel against rifle or machine gun bullets, or bayonet thrusts, although it would have the advantage that there would be no bullet deformation. In the final analysis the report felt that the relative advantages and disadvantages of light body armour could only be properly determined after consultation with surgeons and officers, who had experience of the conditions at the front and knowledge of the relative number of casualties caused by the various types of weapon. Although neither the Dayfield nor the Chemico Body Shields were officially adopted, they clearly influenced the design of the new EOB Body Armour, which was made of 18-gauge manganese steel, heavily padded and covered in tan-coloured canvas.

NOTES

INTRODUCTION

1 Arthur Conan Doyle 1900. *The Great Boer War*, London; Arthur Conan Doyle 1902. *The war in South Africa, its causes and conduct*, London.

2 Arthur Conan Doyle 1913. 'Great Britain and the next war', *Fortnightly Review*, February; anon. 1914. 'Civilian National Reserve', *The Times*, 8 August, 9; anon. 1914. 'Civilian National Reserve', *The Times*, 13 August, 7.

3 Arthur Conan Doyle 1914. 'Lifebelts in men of war', *Daily Mail*, 29 September, 4.

4 Anon. 1914. 'Safety collar for the Navy: new invention ordered for every man', *Daily Express*, 20 October, 5.

5 Arthur Conan Doyle [1915]. Letter to John St Loe Strachey, 6 January. Parliamentary Archives, STR/3/5.

6 Arthur Conan Doyle 1915. 'Life-saving in men-of-war', *Daily Mail*, 6 January, 4; Arthur Conan Doyle 1915. 'Saving our seamen', *Daily Chronicle*, 22 January.

7 William Graham Greene, Permanent Secretary to the Admiralty 1915. Letter to Conan Doyle, 15 January. Royal Armouries, DOY/1/23.

THE FIRST CAMPAIGN, 1915

1 Anon. 1914. 'Steel shields', *Western Mail*, 15 August, 5.

2 Anon. 1914. 'A visit to Przemysl', *Sheffield Independent*, 28 October, 1; anon. 1914. 'New French shield', *Aberdeen Evening Press*, 28 October, 3.

3 Anon. 1915. 'Canadians' spade armour', *Manchester Evening News*, 1 October, 3.

4 Anon. 1915. 'German snipers: British sharpshooters' mastery of them', *Yorkshire Telegraph and Star*, 16 December, 4.

5 Anon. 1914. 'German officers in armour', *Birmingham Mail*, 5 September, 3; anon. 1914. 'Bullet-proof vests', *Yorkshire Telegraph and Star*, 23 November, 3.

6 Anon. 1914. 'A vest of mail', *Birmingham Gazette*, 24 October 1914, 5; anon. 1914. 'Bullet-proof protectors for soldiers charging', *Edinburgh Evening News*, 29 October, 3; anon. 1914. 'Today's news summary', *Hull Daily Mail*, 29 October, 4.

7 Anon., 'Bullet-proof vests'.

8 Anon. 1914. 'Saved by the Kaiser's moustache', *Birmingham Daily Mail*, 22 August, 3.

9 Anon. 1914. 'Birmingham soldier saved by a clip of cartridges', *Birmingham Daily Post*, 17 September, 7.

10 Anon. 1914. 'King chats and jokes with wounded, and hears many stories of remarkable escapes during visit to Chelsea hospital', *Dundee Courier*, 12 October, 4.

11 E. W. Jackson 1914. 'Entrenching tool and shield', GB Patent 21863, 2 November.

12 J. H. T. Greenwood 1915. 'Improvements relating to small arms', GB Patent 1635, 2 February.

13 Mawson, Swan and Morgan Ltd. 1915. Advert, *Newcastle Daily Journal*, 9 February, 4.

14 Patent Office 1915. 'Report of the Comptroller General of Patents, Designs and Trademarks', London.

15 Anon. 1915. 'What the War Office has to put up with. 2, The inventor of the bullet-proof cuirass', *Punch*, 21 April, 317.

16 Anon. 1915. 'Armour for battle: helmets and shields in the trenches', *The Times*, 20 July, 9.

17 Anon. 1915. 'Protection of the skull against wounds by a metallic headpiece', *The Lancet* 185, no. 4790, 1307.

18 Anon. 1915. 'Armoured men: naval surgeon's views', *The Times*, 21 July, 9.

19 A. J. Hewitt 1915. 'Report on the casualties in the action between the Pegasus and the Konigsberg', *Journal of the Royal Naval Medical Service* 1, no. 2, April, 143–54.

20 Anon. 1915, 'Armoured men'.

21 Edward R. Davson 1915. 'Experiments in armour', *The Times*, 22 July, 7.

22 Anon. 1915. 'Trench helmets: a lesson from our allies', *The Times*, 22 July, 5.

23 Anon. 1915. 'Trench armour: question before the authorities', *The Times*, 23 July, 8.

24 Charles ffoulkes 1915. 'Revival of armour, war lessons from the past', *The Times*, 24 July, 9.

25 Desmond O'Callaghan 1915. 'Armour new and old', *The Times*, 26 July, 7.

26 Arthur Conan Doyle 1915. 'The use of armour', *The Times*, 27 July, 7.

27 Arthur Conan Doyle 1900. *The Great Boer War*, London, 176, 520.

28 Moreton Frewen 1915. 'The use of armour', *The Times*, 28 July, 7.

29 Anon. 1915. 'Body plates for soldiers: Sir H. Maxim and armoured soldiers', *Liverpool Echo*, 29 July, 5.

30 Edgar Rathbone 1915. 'Armour and shields', *Spectator*, 7 August, 11.

31 Anon. 1915. 'Conan Doyle wants troops to wear armor', *New York Times*, 27 July, 3.

32 Bashford Dean 1915. 'Should the warrior of today wear armor?', *New York Times Magazine Section*, 19 September, SM4–5.

33 Arthur Conan Doyle 1915. 'Modern armour', *The Times*, 4 August, 7.

34 This appears to have been the mobile shield designed by Lt Cyril Aldin Smith of the Royal Naval Armoured Car Service.

35 The transfer of the War Office Inventions Branch together with its experimental and research establishments finally took place on 29 November 1915; Ministry of Munitions 1922. *History of the Ministry of Munitions*, Vol. II: *General Organisation for Munitions Supply*, Part I: *Administrative Policy and Organisation*, London, 130.

36 Arthur Conan Doyle 1900. 'The War Office and inventors', *The Times*, 22 February, 10; anon. 1900. 'Mr Conan Doyle and high angle fire', *Westminster Gazette*, 26 February.

37 Ernest W. Moir 1915. Letter to Conan Doyle, 27 November. Royal Armouries, DOY/1/1.

38 Col Henry Goold-Adams 1915. Letter to Arthur Conan Doyle, 14 December. Royal Armouries, DOY/1/2.

39 Caleb W. Saleeby 1919. *The whole armour of man: preventive essays for victory in the great campaigns for peace to come*, London, 13.

40 Anon. 1915. 'Six cases where the French shrapnel-proof helmets have saved their wearers' lives', *Daily Mirror*, 13 November, 1.

41 'Lens' [Caleb W. Saleeby] 1915. 'Armoured men', *New Statesman*, 27 November, 177, 178.

42 House of Commons 1915. *Debates*, 14 October, Vol. LXXIV, col. 1494w.

43 House of Commons 1915. *Debates*, 21 October, Vol. LXXIV, col. 2000.

44 Ministry of Munitions 1922. *History of the Ministry of Munitions*, Vol. XI: *The supply of munitions*, Part I: *Trench warfare supplies*, London, 100–2.

45 Anon. 1915. 'Steel shields for soldiers', *The Times*, 3 December, 12.

46 Edward Bagnall Poulton 1915. *Science and the Great War*, London, 42. The Romanes Lecture was delivered at the University Museum on 7 December 1915.

47 Lt Col Maurice A. Hankey, Secretary to the War Council 1922. Memorandum, 28 December 1914, in Ministry of Munitions, *History of the Ministry of Munitions*, Vol. XII: *The supply of munitions*, Part III: *Tanks*, London, 81–2.

48 Winston Churchill, First Lord of the Admiralty 1922. Letter to the Prime Minister, 5 January 1915, in Ministry of Munitions, *Tanks*, 83.

49 Munitions Design Committee, Trench Warfare Section 1916. Minute (T)89, 'Portable shields for infantry', 18 August.

50 Ministry of Munitions 1922. *History of the Ministry of Munitions*, Vol. IX: *Review of munitions supply*, Part II: *Design and inspection*, London, 44–55.

51 Ernest W. Moir 1915. 'Preliminary report on steel bullet-proof shields for use at the front to protect infantry and bombing parties', in Ernest W. Moir, letter to David Lloyd George, 13 August. Parliamentary Archives, LG/D/10/4/1.

52 Ernest W. Moir 1915. 'Further report on steel bullet-proof shields for use at the front to protect infantry and bombing parties', in Ernest W. Moir, letter to David Lloyd George, August 19. Parliamentary Archives, LG/D/10/4/2.

53 Ernest W. Moir 1915. Letter to David Lloyd George, 12 October. Parliamentary Archives, LG/D/10/3/18.

54 David Lloyd George 1915. Memo to Ernest W. Moir, 15 November. Parliamentary Archives, LG/D/3/2/18.

55 Capt. Oliver Lyle 1915. 'Report on armour', 16 November, in Ernest W. Moir, letter to David Lloyd George, 20 November. Parliamentary Archives, LG/D/10/3/25.

56 Capt. Oliver Lyle 1915. 'Report on armour: appended note', 19 November, in Ernest W. Moir, letter to David Lloyd George, 20 November. Parliamentary Archives, LG/D/10/3/25.

57 Ernest W. Moir 1915. Letter to David Lloyd George, 20 November, 20. Parliamentary Archives, LG/D/3/25/1.

58 David Lloyd George 1915. Memo to Maj. Gen. John Philip Du Cane, 29 November. Parliamentary Archives, LG/D/3/2/22.

59 Col Henry Goold-Adams 1915. Letter to David Lloyd George, 16 December. Parliamentary Archives, LG/D/10/3/31.

60 Munitions Design Committee, Trench Warfare Section, 'Portable shields for infantry'.

61 Gen. Douglas Haig, Commander in Chief, British Army in the Field 1915. Letter to the Chief of the Imperial General Staff, War Office, 26 December. The National Archives, MUN 4/2749.

62 David Lloyd George 1916. Memo to Col Henry Goold-Adams, 12 January. Parliamentary Archives, LG/D/3/2/35.

63 The committee consisted of Lt Col Matheson (MD) (Chairman), Maj. the Hon. C. H. Guest (MD), Mr A. McDougall Duckham, Capt. Clark, Capt. Maxwell (from IIS War Office), Capt. Lyle, Lt Symes and Mr W. A. Taylor (Secretary). Munitions Design Committee, Trench Warfare Section 1916. Minute (T)33, 'Shields for infantry', 4 April.

64 Col Henry Goold-Adams 1916. Letter to David Lloyd George, 14 January. Parliamentary Archives, LG/D/10/3/32.

65 Sir Hubert Llewellyn Smith, Secretary, Ministry of Munitions 1916. Letter to the Secretary, War Office, 24 January. The National Archives, MUN 4/2749.

66 Director General Munitions Design 1916. Letter to the Secretary, War Office, 12 February. The National Archives, MUN 4/2749.

THE SECOND CAMPAIGN, 1916–17

1 Percival Phillips 1916. 'Saved by their steel helmets: body armour now suggested for the troops', *Daily Express*, 8 March, 4.

2 Anon., 'Steel helmets at the Front', *Cheltenham Chronicle and Gloucestershire Graphic*, 25 March, 7; 'Lens' [Caleb W. Saleeby] 1916. 'Helmeted heads', *New Statesman*, 15 April, 33–5.

3 Edward Bagnall Poulton 1916. 'Body armour', *The Times*, 12 July, 9.

4 Edward J. Formby 1916. 'Body armour', *The Times*, 17 July, 9.

5 William Frederick de Bois Maclaren 1916. 'Body armour', *The Times*, 18 July, 9.

6 'Wounded in the Push' 1916. 'Body armour', *The Times*, 19 July, 11.

7 'In action' 1916. 'Body armour', *The Times*, 25 July, 9.

8 Edward B. Poulton 1916. 'Body armour', *The Times*, 20 July, 9.

9 Edward B. Poulton 1916. 'Body armour and shields', *The Times*, 29 July, 9.

10 House of Commons 1916. *Debates*, 19 July, Vol. LXXXIV, cols. 1027–1028w.

11 House of Commons 1916. *Debates*, 19 July, Vol. LXXXIV, col. 1384.

12 Arthur Conan Doyle 1916. *A visit of three fronts, June 1916*, London.

13 All of the officers in the 1st Battalion Hampshire Regiment were killed, wounded or missing on 1 July 1916.

14 Arthur Conan Doyle 1916. 'Body armour or shields', *The Times*, 28 July, 9.

15 Poulton, 'Body armour and shields'.

16 W. E. Woodward 1916. 'Body shields', *The Times*, 31 July, 94.

17 Lt Col F. W. M. Newell 1916. 'Body shields', *The Times*, 31 July, 94.

18 Arthur Conan Doyle 1916. 'Body shields: a necessary device', *The Times*, 4 August, 9.

19 Arthur Conan Doyle 1916. 'Body shields and armour: use and limitations, protection against machine gun fire', *Observer*, 6 August, 9.

20 In the published articles the figure for shrapnel is given as 45 per cent, but this is clearly a typographical mistake if the majority of casualties were caused by machine gun fire.

21 Albert Stern 1919. *Tanks, 1914–1918: the log book of a pioneer*, London, 82–3.

22 George Clarke, Lord Sydenham 1916. 'Armour for soldiers: Lord Sydenham considers it impracticable', *Observer*, 13 August, 3.

23 Arthur Conan Doyle 1916. 'Body shields: Sir Conan Doyle replies to a criticism', *Observer*, 20 August, 3.

24 Anon. 1916. Untitled note, *Western Daily Press*, 13 July, 4; anon. 1916. 'The bullet-proof cuirass', *Western Daily Press*, 14 July, 4.

25 Anon. 1916. 'Cotton wool armour for soldiers', *Liverpool Post and Mercury*, 2 August, 6.

26 Anon. 1916. 'Spray of bullets from machine guns: suggested use of steel shield', *The Courier*, 7 August, 5.

27 Anon. 1916. 'Hah Wull has a try at inventing', *Dundee People's Journal*, 26 August, 2.

28 Anon. 1916. 'Steel waistcoat that saved life: new device protects officer who smothered bomb', *Daily Mirror*, 28 July, 11.

29 Anon. 1916. *London Gazette Supplement* 29684, 25 July, 7433; anon. 1916. 'Steel waistcoat saves captain who flung himself on a live bomb to protect seven sleeping men', *Daily Mirror*, 22 August, 1; anon. 1916. 'How a captain's life was saved by his steel waistcoat', *Daily Express*, 22 August, 7.

30 Anon. 1916. 'Saved by a cigarette case', *Daily Mirror*, 7 September, 4.

31 Anon. 1916. 'New life saver', *Shipley Times and Express*, 3 November, 4.

32 Miles Walker 1916. Letter to Arthur Conan Doyle, 4 August. Royal Armouries, DOY/1/8.

33 George Wakeman 1916. Letter to Arthur Conan Doyle, 4 August. Royal Armouries, DOY/1/17.

34 2nd Lt Arthur Rotsaert 1916. Letter to Arthur Conan Doyle, 28 July. Royal Armouries, DOY/1/7.

35 Marthe Durand 1916. Letter to Arthur Conan Doyle, 30 July. Royal Armouries, DOY/ 1/9.

36 John Pullman 1916. Letter to Arthur Conan Doyle, 4 August. Royal Armouries, DOY/1/15.

37 Roneo Ltd 1916. Letter to Arthur Conan Doyle, 5 August. Royal Armouries, DOY/1/19.

38 Janet Peck [1916]. Letter to Arthur Conan Doyle. Royal Armouries, DOY/1/6.

39 Derbyshire Record Office, D4562/8/5.

40 Whitfield Manufacturing Co. Ltd 1916. Letter to Arthur Conan Doyle, 3 August. Royal Armouries, DOY/1/10.

41 Conan Doyle had founded his own miniature rifle club, the Undershaw Rifle Club, at Hindshead in 1902, and the 'Conan Doyle', a challenge statuette first presented by his friend Sir John Langman in 1906, is still competed for every year at the Imperial Meeting held at the National Shooting Centre, Bisley.

42 Arthur Conan Doyle 1924. *Memories and adventures*, 1st edn, London.

43 David Lloyd George 1916. Letter to Arthur Conan Doyle, 31 July. Royal Armouries, DOY/1/3.

44 House of Commons 1916. *Debates*, 31 July, Vol. LXXXIV, col. 2103w.

45 Lt Gen. William Robert Robertson 1916. Letter to Arthur Conan Doyle, 14 August. Royal Armouries, DOY/1/6.

46 Caleb Saleeby 1916. 'Armoured men: the lesson of the helmet', *Liverpool Post and Mercury*, 7 August, 7. Reprinted from the *Daily Post* and *Daily Chronicle*.

47 Anon. 1916. 'A new helmet', *Daily Mirror*, 3 November, 9; 'The Major' 1916. 'Kit chat', *Punch*, 8 November, 326.

48 See note 45 to 'The First Campaign', above. 'Lens' 1916. 'Guarded hearts', *New Statesman*, 12 August, 444.

49 House of Commons 1916. *Debates*, 15 August, Vol. LXXXIV, cols. 1679–705.

50 Caleb Saleeby 1916. 'Body armour: past, present and to come', *Liverpool Post and Mercury*, 28 August, 7. Reprinted from the *Daily Post* and *Daily Chronicle*.

51 'Lens' 1916. 'Further notes on armour', *New Statesman*, 9 September, 541.

52 War Savings Certificates were introduced in June 1916, and cost 15s. 6d. for a £1 certificate.

53 Arthur McDougal Duckham 1916. Memo to Edwin Montagu, 9 August. The National Archives, CAB 1/19/42.

54 Lt Gen. Sir R. C. Maxwell 1916. Letter to the Secretary, War Office, on behalf of the Commander in Chief, British Armies in France, 20 August. The National Archives, MUN 4/2749.

55 Bertram Blakiston Cubbitt, Secretary, War Office 1916. Letter to the Secretary, Ministry of Munitions, 25 August. The National Archives, MUN 4/2749.

56 David Lloyd George 1916. Letter to Arthur Conan Doyle, 2 September. Royal Armouries. DOY/1/2.

57 Arthur Conan Doyle 1916. 'General von Arnim's report', *The Times*, 11 October, 6.

58 Arthur Conan Doyle 1916. Letter to Winston Churchill, 4 October. Churchill Archive, CHAR 2/71/81.

59 House of Commons 1916. *Debates*, 31 October, Vol. LXXXVI, col. 1528.

60 John MacIntosh, Director, Trench Warfare Supply Department 1916. Memo to Director, Munitions Requirements and Statistics, 8 November. The National Archives, MUN 4/2749.

61 Anon. 1916. 'Wounded soldier (seeing a body-shield in a shop window)', *Punch*, 21 October, 308.

62 Caleb Saleeby 1916. 'Saving our soldiers' lives: the triumph of armour', *Liverpool Post and Mercury*, 10 November, 4. Reprinted from the *Daily Chronicle*.

63 House of Commons 1916. *Debates*, 22 November, Vol. LXXXVII, col. 1435w.

64 Anon. 1917. 'Devices for protecting our soldiers: what the steel helmet would withstand', *Birmingham Daily Post*, 13 March, 8.

65 'Lens' 1917. 'Armour in 1917', *New Statesman*, 31 March, 609–10.

66 Anon. 1917. 'Modern forms of medieval armour', *Manchester Guardian*, 19 July, 4.

67 Frances Stevenson 1917. *Lloyd George: a diary*, A. J. P. Taylor (ed.), London, 142.

68 Conan Doyle, *Memories and adventures*, 381–4 (383).

69 Arthur Conan Doyle 1917. 'His last bow: the war service of Sherlock Holmes', *Strand Magazine*, September. Collected in Arthur Conon Doyle 1917. *His last bow: some reminiscences of Sherlock Holmes*, London.

70 War Cabinet 1917. 'Minutes of a meeting of the War Cabinet held on 22 March 1917'. The National Archives, CAB 23/2/20.

71 Secretary of State for War 1917. 'Body armour: memorandum by the Secretary of State for War', 14 April. The National Archives, CAB 24/10/56.

72 Secretary of State for War 1917. 'Body armour: memorandum by the Secretary of State for War', 19 June. The National Archives, CAB 24/16/98.

73 William A. Taylor 1917. Letter to the Comptroller, MID, 23 February. The National Archives, MUN 5/119/700/6.

74 House of Commons 1918. *Debates*, 18 February, Vol. CIII, col. 487w.

75 House of Commons 1918. *Debates*, 28 May, Vol. CVI, col. 650.

76 Saleeby, *The whole armour of man*, 358.

77 Captain I. St Rose 1918. 'Armour: conclusions from experiments etc.', 13 September. Metropolitan Museum of Art, Bashford Dean Archives.

78 Lt Col O. F. Brothers, 'The development of weapons used in trench warfare'. The National Archives MUN 5/383.

CONCLUSION

1 Ministry of Munitions 1922. *History of the Ministry of Munitions*, Vol. XI: *The supply of munitions*, Part II: *Trench warfare supplies*, London, 104.
2 Arthur Conan Doyle 1924. *Memories and adventures*, 1st edn, London, 385.
3 Caleb W. Saleeby 1919. *The whole armour of man: preventive essays for victory in the great campaigns for peace to come*, London, 358.

POSTSCRIPT

1 Bashford Dean 1915. 'Should the warrior of today wear armor?', *New York Times Magazine Section*, 19 September, SM4–5.
2 Capt. A. J. Simonds, Ordnance Department 1917. 'Memorandum to Major Simpson: 'Information needed from abroad', 17 October. Metropolitan Museum of Art, Bashford Dean Archives.
3 Donald J. La Rocca 2014. 'Bashford Dean and helmet design during World War I', 23 July, www. metmuseum.org/blogs/now-at-the-met/2014/bashford-dean-and-helmet-design-during-world-war-i (accessed 2 May 2017).
4 Bashford Dean 1920. *Helmets and body armor in modern warfare*, New Haven.

APPENDIX I

1 Ministry of Munitions 1922. *History of the Ministry of Munitions*, Vol. IX: *Review of munitions supply*, Part II: *Design and inspection*, London, 58.
2 A fourth condition, that the body shield should not exceed a weight of 15 lb, was added at a later date.
3 TWS 1916. Minute (T)7, 'Shields for bombers', 27 January.
4 TWS 1916. Minute (T)12, 'Shields for bombers', 15 February.
5 TWS 1916. Minute (T)92, 'Shields for bombers', 8 August.
6 TWS 1916. Minute (T)89, 'Portable shields for infantry', 18 August.
7 Woodite was a tradename for an elastic packing material of fibrous character and consisting in part of india rubber.
8 TWS 1916. Minute (T)6, 'Portable shields for infantry', 27 January.
9 TWS 1916. Minute (T)11, 'Portable shields for infantry', 15 February.
10 TWS 1916. Minute (T)89.
11 TWS 1916. Minute (T)33, 'Portable fields for infantry', 4 April.
12 TWS 1916. Minute (T)103, 'Shields for Infantry', 27 October.
13 Bashford Dean 1920. *Helmets and body armor in modern warfare*, New Haven, 1920, 174–6.
14 Brig. Gen. J. Bennett Stuart 1916. Letter to the Secretary, War Office, on behalf of the Commander in Chief, British Armies in France, 7 October. The National Archives, MUN 4/2749.
15 Capt. W. D. Clark 1916. Memo to Captain Ley, on behalf of the Comptroller of Munitions Inventions, 19 December. The National Archives, MUN 4/2749.
16 TWS 1916. Minute (T)42, 'Shields on wheels', 27 April.
17 TWS 1916. Minute (T)44, 'Pedrail shield', 27 April.

1 Frances Dayton and Ernest Albert Whitfield 1915. 'Improvements in or relating to shields for the use of soldiers and others', GB Patent 5196, 6 April; David Anderson 1915. 'Improvements in or relating to shields for the use of soldiers and others', GB Patent 17333, 18 December.

2 Whitfield Manufacturing Co. Ltd. 1916. Promotional leaflet for the Dayfield Body Shield. Royal Armouries DOY/1/10.

3 Sir Hubert Llewellyn Smith, Secretary, Ministry of Munitions 1916. Letter to the Secretary, War Office, 24 January. The National Archives, MUN 4/2749.

4 David Anderson 1916. 'Improvements in or relating to shields or protectors suitable for the use of soldiers and others', GB Patent 103140, 7 January.

5 Lt Gen. Sir R. C. Maxwell 1916. Letter to the Secretary, War Office, on behalf of the Commander in Chief, British Armies in France, 20 August. The National Archives, MUN 4/2749.

6 Anon. 1916. Photo, *Illustrated London News*, 22 July, 108.

7 Anon. 1916. 'Body shield for soldiers: interesting tests in Birmingham', *Birmingham Daily Post*, 9 May, 3; anon. 1916. 'A new body shield', *Army and Navy Gazette*, 6 May, 13.

8 Wilfrid Hill and Joseph Percy Wilks 1917. 'Improvements in bullet-proof and like garments, and in coverings for horses and articles exposed to acts of warfare', GB Patent 104699, 10 February; 110093, 14 February.

9 William A. Taylor 1917. Letter to the Comptroller, Munitions Inventions Department, 23 February. The National Archives, MUN 5/119.

10 William Beedle 1916. 'Improvements relating to shields for personal wear', GB Patent 104911, 21 March.

SELECT BIBLIOGRAPHY

ROYAL ARMOURIES, CONAN DOYLE CORRESPONDENCE

DOY 1/1, Ernest Moir, Comptroller, Munitions Inventions Department, letter, 27 November 1915.

DOY 1/2, Col Henry Goold-Adams, Acting Comptroller, Munitions Inventions Department, letter, 14 December 1915..

DOY 1/3, David Lloyd George, Secretary of State for War, letter, 31 July 1916.

DOY 1/4, Lt Gen. Sir William Robertson, Chief of the Imperial General Staff, letter, 14 August 1916.

DOY 1/5, David Lloyd George, Secretary of State for War, letter, 2 December 1916.

DOY 1/6, Janet Peck, letter, no date.

DOY 1/7, Lt Arthur Rotsaert, Royal Belgian Engineers, letter, 28 July 1916.

DOY 1/8, H. Chatel, letter, 30 July 1916.

DOY 1/9, Marthe Durand, letter, 30 July 1916.

DOY 1/10, Whitfield Manufacturing Company, letter with promotional material, 3 August 1916.

DOY 1/11, J. Davies, letter, 4 August 1916.

DOY 1/12, J. B. Forster, letter, 4 August 1916.

DOY 1/13, A. Middleton, letter, 4 August 1916.

DOY 1/14, Capt. Philippe Millet, letter, 4 August 1916.

DOY 1/15, John Pullman, letter with promotional material, 4 August 1916.

DOY 1/16, George Seaborn, letter, 4 August 1916.

DOY 1/17, George Wakeman, letter, 4 August 1916.

DOY 1/18, Professor Miles Walker, Victoria University of Manchester, letter with photographs, 4 August 1916.

DOY 1/19, Roneo Ltd, letter with drawings and promotional material, 5 August 1916.

DOY 1/20, Magazine article, 'The Daigre bullet-proof shield', *The Field*, 5 August 1916.

DOY 1/21, J. R. Cohu, letter to Mrs Conan Doyle, 9 September 1916.

DOY 1/22, William Graham Greene, Permanent Secretary to the Admiralty, letter, 14 January 1915.

THE NATIONAL ARCHIVES, KEW

CAB 1/19/42, Cabinet Office, miscellaneous records, 'Protection offered by body armour', 9 August 1916.

CAB 23/2/20, War Cabinet, minutes, 22 March 1917.

CAB 24/10/56, War Cabinet, 'Body armour', memorandum by the Secretary of State for War, 14 April 1917.

CAB 24/16/98, War Cabinet, 'Body armour', memorandum by the Secretary of State for War, 19 June 1917.

MUN 4/135, Ministry of Munitions, records of the Central Registry, 'Inventions and suggestions: shields', 21 May–5 July 1915.

MUN 4/2749, Ministry of Munitions, records of the Central Registry, research, 'Portable bullet shields and body shields: trials', 26 December 1915–26 January 1917.

MUN 4/3281, War Cabinet, copies of War Cabinet minutes concerning shipping losses from sub-marine attack and food supply; manpower for construction of ships and marine engines; shipping supplies to Russia; body armour, 1917.

MUN 5/119/700/6, Munitions Council, Historical Records Branch, monthly reports on work of Inventions Department, nos. 3–38, 30 November 1915–13 December 1918.

MUN 5/383/1600/4, Munitions Council, Historical Records Branch, 'Development of weapons used in trench warfare', December 1918–December 1919.

MUN 7/288, Munitions Inventions Department, 'Invention of, or suggestions for:– armour-piercing bullets and body armour', 15 January 1917–2 March 1918.

MUN 9/21, Lloyd George Papers, 'Inventions: coordination of Ministry of Munitions and War Office activities', July–November 1915.

WO 140/15, School of Musketry, Hythe, reports of trials with arms, ammunition etc., nos. 330–45, 29 April 1914–14 September 1915.

WO 140/15, School of Musketry, Hythe, reports of trials with arms, ammunition etc., nos. 454–89, 491–547 and unnumbered, 23 September 1915–6 December 1916.

PARLIAMENTARY ARCHIVES, DAVID LLOYD GEORGE PAPERS

LG/D/3/2/5, David Lloyd George, memo to Dr Christopher Addison, Parliamentary Secretary, including the testing of breastplates on sale at the Junior Army and Navy Stores, undated.

LG/D/3/2/18, David Lloyd George, memo to Sir Frederick Black, Director General of Munitions Supply, 15 November 1915.

LG/D/3/2/21, David Lloyd George, memo to Ernest Moir, Controller of Munitions Inventions Department, 15 November 1915 (same as LG/D/3/2/18).

LG/D/3/2/22, David Lloyd George, memo to General de Cane, Director General of Munitions Design, regarding items to discuss at a meeting, including item 6, armoured protection for men, 29 November 1915.

LG/D/3/2/35, David Lloyd George, letter to Col Goold-Adams, Controller of Munitions Inventions Department, regarding the prospects of securing body shields, and asking for a report on the Dayfield Body Shield, 12 January 1916.

LG/D/3/25/1, Ernest Moir, Controller of Munitions Inventions Department, letter to David Lloyd George, 20 November 1915.

LG/D/10/3/4, Ernest Moir, Controller of Munitions Inventions Department, letter to David Lloyd George including a report on shields, 11 August 1915.

LG/D/10/3/5, Ernest Moir, Controller of Munitions Inventions Department, letter to David Lloyd George noting that he was enclosing a report on shields (not in file), 12 August 1915.

LG/D/10/3/18, Ernest Moir, Controller of Munitions Inventions Department, letter to David Lloyd George including a long report, and noting a new design for a shield, 12 October 1915.

LG/D/10/3/25, Ernest Moir, Controller of Munitions Inventions Department, letter to David Lloyd George enclosing a report on tests on shields purchased from the Junior Army and Navy Stores, 20 November 1915.

LG/D/10/3/31, Col Goold-Adams, Controller of Munitions Inventions Department, letter to David Lloyd George regarding the sub-committee on body armour, 16 December 1915.

LG/D/10/3/32, Col Goold-Adams, Controller of Munitions Inventions Department, report to David Lloyd George containing the findings of the sub-committee on body armour, 14 January 1916.

LG/D/10/4/1, Ernest Moir, Controller of Munitions Inventions Department, letter to David Lloyd George enclosing a report on body armour, 13 August 1915.

LG/D/10/4/2, Ernest Moir, Controller of Munitions Inventions Department, letter to David Lloyd George containing a supplementary report, 19 August 1915.

STR/33/5, Sir Arthur Conan Doyle, letters to John St Loe Strachey, editor of the *Spectator*.

METROPOLITAN MUSEUM OF ART, BASHFORD DEAN ARCHIVE

The Bashford Dean Archive, relating to his work on helmets and body armour during the First World War and his book on helmets and modern body armour, is currently uncatalogued. The following is only a small part of the complete papers relating to his visit to Europe, and his discussions with the Munitions Inventions Department, together with a selection of other documents.

Dean, Bashford, 'Enquiry in regard to use of armour', January 1918.

Dean, Bashford, 'Latest results of European specialists', 26 February 1918.

Dean, Bashford, letter to W. A. Taylor, Munitions Inventions Department, 26 November 1918.

Dean, Bashford, memorandum of correspondence received, 3 December 1917.

Dean, Bashford 'Net results of mission abroad', [December 1917].

Dean, Bashford, 'Preliminary report on helmets and body armor', December 1917.

Dean, Bashford, two pocket books containing notes on his mission to Europe, November–December 1917.

General Head Quarters, 'American Expeditionary Force: heavy and light body armour', 19 October 1917.

General Head Quarters, 'American Expeditionary Force: policy as regards body armour', 3 January 1918.

General Head Quarters, 'American Expeditionary Force: proceedings of a Board of Officers … for the purpose of conducting a series of tests on articles of body armor, helmets and other devices submitted by the Ordnance Department', 23 April 1918.

Lassiter, Gen. William, 'Information on military protective apparatus which has been tried out by the British Government in actual service', 19 October 1917.

Ley, Capt. C. H., 'Data obtained from the Ministry of Munitions of Capt. C. H. Ley, re. helmets and body armour', November 1917.

Ley, Capt. C. H., 'Tests of silk: notes on tests carried out by Capt. C. H. Ley, Munitions Inventions Department', November 1917.

Munitions Inventions Department, 'Answers from the Munitions Inventions Department and Trench Warfare Supply Department to questions asked by the Ordnance Bureau in the matters of helmets and body armor', November 1917.

Munitions Inventions Department, 'Deflection of bullets from armour plates', 24 May 1917.

Munitions Inventions Department, 'Experimental work of Mr Taylor', December 1917.

Munitions Inventions Department, 'Notes on body armour', 2 August 1916.

Phillips, William, US Secretary of State for War, letter to Bashford Dean, 3 August 1917.

St Rose, Capt. I., Trench Warfare Department, 'Armour conclusions from experiments', 18 September 1918.

St Rose, Capt. I., Trench Warfare Department, 'Report on armour', 15 November 1917.

Taylor, W. A., 'Ballistic value of various materials: notes on tests carried out by W. A. Taylor, Munitions Inventions Department', November 1917.

Taylor, W. A., Munitions Inventions Department, 'Notes on experiments and suggestions that have been made in connection with light armour', 4 September 1917.

Taylor, W. A. Munitions Inventions Department, 'Notes on the penetration of armour plates', 11 March 1919.

Taylor, W. A., 'Shields: notes on tests carried out by W. A. Taylor, Munitions Inventions Department', November 1917.

US Bureau of Standards, memorandum, 19 October 1917.

US Ordnance Department, Equipment Division, trench warfare material, 2 November 1917.
US Ordnance Department, memorandum to Maj. Simpson, 17 October 1917.

PUBLISHED SOURCES

Dean, Bashford 1920. *Helmets and body armor in modern warfare*, New York.
Saunders, Anthony 1999. *Weapons of trench warfare, 1914–1918*, Stroud.
Saunders, Anthony 2012. *Reinventing warfare, 1914–1918: novel munitions and tactics of trench warfare*, London.